"Hope" is a thing with feathers—
That perches in the soul—
And sings the tune without words,
And never stops—at all.

—Emily Dickinson

How To B unce When Others Break

The Top 10 Rules of Resilient People

Dr. Steve W. Price
Author of Bestseller "Household Gold"

M ETAPHOR PRESS

How to Bounce When Others Break
by Dr. Steve W. Price

Metaphor Press
10427 Orange Grove Dr.
Tampa, FL 33618

Distributed exclusively through:
Kat Ranch Marketing
140 S. Main Street
Brooksville, FL 34601

ISBN: 978-0-9822549-2-9
Published by Metaphor Press

Printed in United States of America
Cover design and text layout by Parry Design Studio, Inc.

DEDICATION

To Carol, resilient beyond belief

BEST-SELLING BOOKS
BY DR. STEVE W. PRICE

Dream Making in a Dream-Taking World

Household Gold

WWW. Stands for 'World Wide Whiners'

Surviving the Perfect Recession

CONTENTS

"Resilient People Are Like Trees Bending in the Wind."

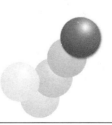

"Resilient People Are Like Trees Bending in the Wind."

I'm a little wounded, but I am not slain.
I will lay me down for to bleed awhile.
Then I'll rise and fight again.
—John Dryden
English poet

"**E**verybody is in pain," lamented the raspy baritone voice on my car radio. "We're all hurting. Some of us a little. Some a lot. But we're all in some kind of pain. So be nice to people."

The words came from Dennis Prager, a widely syndicated conservative talk radio host, during one of his recent three-hour daily broadcasts.

His words hit me like a bolt from the blue.

I steered my car to a side street and swung into an empty parking lot. I switched off the radio and sat in silence, pondering that simple but powerful statement.

Everybody is in pain. Some a little. Some a lot.

Prager is spot on—pain is the human condition. It cuts across cultures and customs and colors. It's with us all our waking hours. Obviously, it varies in degree—some are in a little pain, some a lot—and in type: Pain can be physical... emotional... financial... familial... or mental. But we're all touched by pain—sometimes racked by pain—day in and day out.

Life: a Course in Pain Management

Because pain is a given in our lives, the question isn't how to avoid pain because it's unavoidable. The question is, *how do we best manage pain so we can keep moving forward with our lives?*

Some people experience tremendous, unrelenting pain and still manage to remain amazingly productive, such as British physicist Dr. Stephen Hawking, who has written numerous books, even though he has been virtually paralyzed by Lou Gehrig's disease (ALS) for nearly 40 years. (Contrast that with nightly TV reports of young rich, pampered celebrities who overdose on prescription drugs at the sight of their first wrinkle.)

So, what is it that makes some people so resilient that they can bounce back from seemingly unbearable pain... while others break like an egg dropped on a marble floor at the slightest bump in the road?

This book seeks to answer that question by identifying the *top 10 rules of resilient people.* These rules empower people to manage their pain... to rise above it, and, in many cases, to use their pain to launch themselves to even greater achievements.

What Is Resilience?

Resiliency—the choice to bend, not break—has been a hot research topic among psychologists since 9/11 and has gained momentum during the first decade of the 21st century as people have been forced to face a long list of disruptions and disasters: wars in Iraq and Afghanistan... Hurricane Katrina... the tsunami in Indonesia... the earthquake in Haiti... and the deepest global recession since the Great Depression, costing taxpayers trillions of dollars, sending millions of people into unemployment lines, and forcing hundreds of thousands of homeowners into foreclosures.

This is not a good time to be emotionally brittle.

The word "resilience" comes from an ancient French word meaning "to leap or jump; to spring back into shape after being compressed, bent, or stretched." Over the centuries, the word resilience has evolved to mean, "to recover strength, spirits, and good humor."

Resilient people have the ability to rebound quickly from a crisis or trauma. They call upon some inner belief system and employ success strategies that enable them to process their pain and keep moving forward, instead of falling apart and shattering like a pane of glass when faced with adversity. "Resilient people are like trees bending in the wind. They bounce back," says Dr. Steven Southwick, professor of psychiatry at Yale University School of Medicine.

A Tale of Two Weddings

Dr. Southwick has coined a phrase to describe resilient people who not only overcome misfortune but who also convert adversity into opportunity. He calls this phenomenon "post-traumatic *growth* syndrome," a positive play on the much-media-discussed "post-traumatic *stress* syndrome."

People displaying post-traumatic *growth* syndrome put a positive spin on negative events, seeing them as an opportunity to better themselves and become better people.

"You can get better, or you can get bitter," goes the old expression. People who choose to get better bounce. People who choose to get bitter break. It's as simple as that.

I'd like to take a moment to tell you two brief stories. The first story personifies a person in pain getting bitter and breaking. The second personifies the opposite, getting better and bouncing. Both stories begin with the same event—a bride left at the altar. But the responses of the two brides-to-be couldn't be more different.

The first story involves one of the most famous characters in fiction, Miss Havisham from Charles Dickens' classic novel, *Great Expectations*. At 20 minutes to nine on her wedding day, while she was still dressing, Miss Havisham received a letter from her intended stating he was not going through with the ceremony. Heartbroken and humiliated, Miss Havisham froze her pain in time by stopping all the clocks at the exact time she received the letter of rejection. She remained in her room for the last 30-plus years of her life, never removing her wedding gown and leaving the uneaten wedding cake on the table. She gains her revenge on men by adopting an orphan, Estella, and raising her daughter to become an ice princess, enticing men with her looks and charm only to break their hearts. By the end of the novel, Miss Havisham is a brittle, broken woman, literally. Her dress is yellowed and tattered and her skin thin and wrinkled from lack of sun. She dies when her long dress brushes an ember in the fireplace and her dry, brittle dress bursts into flames.

Unlike the tale of Dickens' fictional Miss Havisham, the second story happened to a real woman, Teanne Harris. Miss Harris' fiancée got cold feet only six days before the scheduled wedding. Discovering it was too late for a refund for the reception, Miss Harris decided to turn her wedding reception into a holiday party for 340 residents of the nearby Asbury Court Retirement Community. Although she didn't know any of the residents, she moved everything to the reception room in Asbury Court—food, flowers, table decorations, even the DJ.

"I worked really hard on planning for the perfect party," Miss Harris said, "and it would have broken my heart even more to have it go to waste. The residents helped me out by giving me some joy watching them enjoy the food, the setting... and even the music."

What Can You Learn from This Book?

We're all faced with two choices when it comes to dealing with pain in our lives. We can choose to become a *victim* and let pain run our lives—and possibly *ruin* our lives, like Miss Havisham. Or we can choose to become a *victor* by triumphing over pain, like Miss Harris.

Better to bounce like Harris than break like Havisham, wouldn't you agree? That's what this book is all about—learning the strategies (I call them rules) that resilient people use to bounce back from adversity.

This book will describe the 10 key strategies that resilient people use to process pain, pick themselves up, and, like the mythical phoenix birds that die a fiery death and are magically reborn from the ashes, to soar once again. These rules will help you bounce back from not only the daily nuisance pains that wear on us like a steady rain on a rock, such as sullen kids… or demanding bosses… or unexpected expenses; but these rules can also help us rebound from spirit-crushing pain, such as living with a chronic disease… losing a home to bankruptcy… struggling to save a sinking business… or, even worse, losing a loved one.

Strategies for Coping with Adversity

Psychologists have a term that sums up the master key to resiliency. Behavioral experts call it "active coping," and it's the opposite of remaining frozen by trauma, a permanent captive of pain.

"Resilient people quickly zero in on challenges and devise strategies for dealing with them, whether it's asking for help… seeking out resources… learning new skills… or striking out on novel paths," says *Psychology Today*. "They call on their inner strength and recruit outside resources to keep moving forward, and they tweak their future expectations to fit their new reality, be it the loss of a loved one, a life-changing diagnosis, or a devastating financial blow."

I've broken down the strategy of active coping into the "Top Ten Rules of Resilient People." These rules have helped millions of people not only to bounce back from adversity, but, in many cases, to turn adversity into advantage.

The top 10 rules discussed in the following pages are designed to help you bend in the wind so that you can bask in the sunshine once the storm passes.

RESILIENT RULE 1:

Read the Writing on the Wall

Read the Writing on the Wall

The time to deal with denial is right now, this very day. Don't wait for a crisis. It will be too late.
—Richard Tedlow
Author, *Denial*

Henry Ford and King Belshazzar of Babylonia lived thousands of years apart, but they both had one thing in common that led to disaster.

They couldn't read the writing on the wall.

Let's start with the story of Belshazzar, from which the expression, "read the writing on the wall" originated.

While participating in a drunken palace feast, King Belshazzar of Babylon used sacred cups and vessels plundered from Solomon's Temple to propose toasts and sing praises to his pagan gods. Immediately, a supernatural, floating hand wrote several words on the palace wall. The king's astronomers and magicians couldn't decode the strange script, so the king sent for Daniel, an exiled Jew, who recognized the Hebrew script and interpreted the words to mean that God had weighed the king's transgressions and decreed his dynasty and his days on earth were coming to an end.

That night, Belshazzar was murdered and his kingdom divided.

Ford Puts on the Blinders

Henry Ford's failure to "read the writing on the wall" was figurative rather than literal, but it led to the near-death of the company he founded in 1903, Ford Motor Company.

After perfecting the assembly line, Ford dominated car sales by churning out a million new cars a year at a price the working man could afford. Ford's philosophy was to give the public the best value by offering a black box with few frills. "Any customer can have a Ford painted any color he wants as long as it's black," Ford famously quipped. By 1918, one of every two cars on the road was a Ford. The proud, headstrong Henry Ford thought he and his company were invincible.

But as the country prospered, consumers started demanding more than a black box. Yes, buyers wanted more colors. But they also wanted more variety. More comfort. And more features. Even if they had to pay extra to get them.

General Motors read the writing on the wall. By the late 1920s, GM offered five brands—Cadillac, Pontiac, Buick, Oldsmobile, and Chevrolet—in an array of colors and new designs every few years. GM sales soared as Ford's sales slipped.

Henry Ford ignored the writing on the wall, saying the Model T, basically unchanged in two decades, was fine. He attributed the slip in market share to an incompetent sales force. Frustrated workers tried to persuade the flinty Ford to modernize the Model T by surprising him with a sleek, customized version of the "tin Lizzie" upon his return from a vacation. Ford thanked them by kicking in the front windshield and jumping up and down on the roof and hood.

The Model T stayed the same.

When sales of the Model T plummeted in 1927, Ford finally relented. He shut down the main manufacturing plant and sent the workers home. The company that sold 15 million Model Ts was on the brink of bankruptcy.

Denial Is Not a River in Egypt

The expression "the writing on the wall" refers to ominous signs or megatrends that inevitably lead to misfortune or doom. These signs are so obvious that anyone with average intelligence and a trace of common sense can see them.

Yet, even very smart people, like Henry Ford in the 1920s and Ivy League-educated Wall Street bankers in the months and years leading up to the 2008 crash, missed these obvious portents of misfortune.

Why do so many people fail to read the writing on the wall?

Two reasons—ignorance or denial.

Let's start with **ignorance**. In this day and age, with information available 24/7 at the touch of a keyboard, *claiming ignorance as an excuse just doesn't fly anymore.* Cigarette smokers who get lung cancer, for example, may testify to a jury that they were ignorant of the dangers of smoking, but they aren't ignorant—they're lying. Even back in the 1930s and '40s, when cigarette smoking was glamorized in the movies and even doctors endorsed certain brands, cigarettes were nicknamed "cancer sticks" and "coffin nails." People have always known the dangers of smoking—smokers have just chosen to pretend that inhaling cigarette smoke won't affect their heart or lungs... until it inevitably does.

Which leads us to **denial**, the second, and biggest, reason people fail to read the writing on the wall. In his book *Denial: Why Business Leaders Fail to Look Facts in the Face—and What to Do About It*, author Richard Tedlow defines denial as "the unwillingness to see or admit a truth that ought to be apparent and is in fact apparent to many others." He goes on to say that denial "may be the biggest and potentially the most ruinous problem that businesses face, from startups to mature, powerful corporations."

In short, groups, as well as individuals, see what they *wish* to see, as opposed to what is. If the writing on the wall runs contrary to people's best interests, more often than not, they ignore it.

Resilient People Read—and Heed—the Warning Signs

Let's take a moment to look at some resilient people who bounced, while others broke, because they studied the gathering storm clouds while the masses were still wearing sunglasses.

The first story may take you back to your childhood if your parents read *Curious George* books to you at bedtime, as mine did. George is a lovable monkey whose curiosity gets him into all kinds of troubling situations, but, by the end of each of the 36 books, George manages to escape disaster and return home to his owner, known only as "the man with a big yellow hat."

First published in the U.S. in 1941, the *Curious George* series has remained in print for 60 years and has sold 30 million copies in dozens of languages. The original seven books were written and illustrated by a husband and wife team, Margaret and H.A. Rey, and their real-life adventure parallels the narrow escapes of their fictional friend.

Born in Germany, Margaret and Hans Rey were Jews living in Paris on the eve of the Nazi invasion of France. Twice in the months leading up to the invasion, French police sympathetic to the Germans questioned the couple. Duly warned, the Reys scavenged and bartered for used bike parts, eventually patching together two rickety bikes. Two days before the Germans marched into the city, the couple fled on their homemade bicycles carrying a knapsack with drawings and stories for their children's books, including one about a curious monkey named Fifi, later changed to George. They made the 900-mile trip to Lisbon in nine days, sleeping in barns during the day and bicycling at night. The couple eventually made their way to London, where they begged and borrowed money to sail to America.

To Bounce, You Must Act

A similar story happened to a real-life George, a friend of mine who escaped from Hungary in the days following the failed 1956 Hungarian Revolution. As an 18-year-old college freshman in Budapest, George took part in the protest march and spontaneous riots that broke out in the capital city on October 23. He passed out flyers demanding freedom from Soviet rule and was active in making bombs to attack the hated secret police. At first the Soviets gave in to student demands, loosening their grip on Hungary and installing a president sympathetic to reforms. But fearful the nascent rebellion would spread to other occupied countries in Eastern Europe, the Soviet leadership cracked down hard on the Hungarian dissidents, sending a thousand armored tanks and 30,000 troops into Budapest.

George knew his days in Hungary were numbered. At best he'd be sent to a Russian concentration camp; at worst he'd face a firing squad. He read the writing on the wall and made plans to flee the country. Recognizing that the Soviets would concentrate on securing the cities first, George and three of his best childhood friends escaped over a rugged mountain range into Austria. George worked and saved money to pay smugglers to guide his parents and younger brother through the heavily mined border to join him in Austria. George's family and three best buddies all eventually relocated to the United States, where they all took advantage of their newfound freedom and free enterprise to open and operate successful businesses.

All told, 200,000 of the 10 million Hungarian citizens escaped to the West in the months following the October 23 riots. The rebels who didn't act by fleeing were put on trial. Within weeks the Soviets imprisoned 40,000 Hungarians for treason; the 400 most visible leaders were executed by firing squad, and hundreds more "disappeared" and were never heard from again.

Today George is comfortably retired in a modern three-story home (designed by one of the childhood friends who escaped with George in '56) fronting the Intracoastal Waterway in St. Pete Beach, Florida.

He's still active in business and active in the lives of his three children and several grandchildren.

All the result of following Resilience Rule #1: Read the Writing on the Wall—and then ACTING accordingly.

My Story: Tough Love for a Defiant Daughter

We're all faced with tough choices in our lives, but the choices are even tougher when they're close to home, especially when it comes to your children.

But resilient people don't ignore the writing on the wall just because it criticizes the person they love the most in this world. In my case, the writing communicated a message about my daughter, Sydney. Here's our story:

My daughter is a good kid. She has a lot going for her. She's pretty. Smart. Funny. Outgoing. But, like a lot of high schoolers, she hadn't developed a strong sense of self. In the second half of her junior year, she distanced herself from her volleyball buddies and started hanging around with a faster group of friends. Her grades slipped. Her attitude became more sullen and oppositional. In short, she wasn't the Sydney I knew anymore. She was becoming the Sydney her rebellious friends were telling her to become.

I used to teach high school, and I'd seen some tragic things happen to some really great kids who migrated to the wrong peer group. Syd's mom and I couldn't ignore her downward-spiraling behavior anymore. We agreed to take drastic action.

On the Fourth of July, 2008, the summer before Sydney's senior year in high school, we sat down with our daughter and told her we were enrolling her in a 28-day therapeutic wilderness camp in North Carolina. She ended up spending two months camping and hiking in a wilderness park near Asheville. She learned a lot about survival skills, but more importantly, a lot about herself, and on our final visit, I could tell she'd done some growing up.

But she had a lot more growing to do before she could start making better choices. So, that fall we enrolled our only daughter into The Oakley School, a therapeutic boarding school near a small mountain town 20 minutes from Park City, Utah. From September 2008 until her graduation in August 2009, we saw Sydney only three times.

Did we miss her? Yes and no.

I missed the silly, smiling Sydney with a good heart and messy room. But I didn't miss the sassy, sullen Sydney that was turning her back on her true nature and allowing some sour, self-centered teenagers to reshape her into their image.

From Plan A... to Plan Z

Sending our daughter away for her senior year of high school was not in our plans. Even at the start of summer vacation, our plan was to enjoy watching her play high school and club volleyball... snapping her homecoming and prom photos... eating pizza and watching Audrey Hepburn movies on the weekends.

But when the writing on the wall got bigger and bolder, Plan A jumped to Plan Z in a matter of weeks. We went from savoring our last few months with our daughter at home to sending her into exile 2,000 miles away to a therapeutic boarding school specializing in putting errant high school kids back on the right path.

It was the right decision for Sydney.

But it was the hardest decision I ever made.

I'll never forget my moment of truth. We were visiting Oakley on September 11, 2008. We took a tour of The Oakley School, a rustic lodge set in a wildflower-strewn valley in the Wasatch Mountain Range, a half-hour drive from Salt Lake City.

Syd's mom and I were impressed. Sydney was not.

Because she was 18, Sydney had to sign off on attending the school.

"No way am I going to this place," she huffed. "I hate it."

The admissions officer asked Sydney to leave so she could talk openly with the parents.

"Well," I said, "we can't force her to go here because she is 18, and there's no way she's voluntarily attending this school. So now what?"

"If you give your daughter the choice of staying here or going home, she'll choose going home," said the admissions officer. "But there is another therapeutic boarding school 90 miles from here called Turn Around Ranch. The students there get up at 5 a.m. every day, seven days a week. It's a working ranch, so by 5:30 they're cleaning horse barns, mending fences, mowing lawns, and feeding hogs. They go to school five hours a day and work five hours a day. Students who transfer from the ranch to Oakley say this place is a resort compared to the ranch. I suggest you give her a choice: Oakley or the ranch, but make it clear that going home is NOT an option."

Truth is, I was hoping someone at Oakley would pull out some obscure law that said 18-year-olds were NOT legally adults in Utah, making Oakley officials in charge of the decision. No such law existed, so it was up to Syd's mom and me to tell her she could choose Oakley… or she could choose Turn Around Ranch. But going home was not a choice. End of discussion.

You Can Ignore the Writing, but You Can't Erase It

If you're a parent, you understand the instinct to shelter your kids from pain, not inflict it. So, when you hear a crying, hysterical teenager begging to come home… swearing they will change if you give them just one more chance… accusing you of ruining their life "because you're selfish and don't want me around anymore"—well, your first reaction is to erase the pain.

You can ignore the writing on the wall, *but you cannot erase it.*

And the writing told us we had one last chance to redirect our child.

Sydney stayed and graduated from Oakley.

I'd be the first to say that I'm not a particularly courageous person, but truth is, it takes a bit of courage to become resilient... to face the facts and do something about it. It's easy to be passive and just let the world push you along, even if it means you're being pushed over a cliff. It took courage for the Reys and my friend George to escape from imminent disaster. But the truth is, thousands of Jews in Paris... and millions in Hungary... saw the writing on the wall, but less than 1% tried to escape.

What about the Writing on Your Wall?

We're all confronted with the writing on the wall, and that writing is always personal and it never goes away until either we act on it or it acts on us.

Take a moment to read the writing on the wall of your life. You know it's there. If you've been ignoring it, you're preparing yourself to break when you could be bouncing.

Maybe the writing is warning you about your child's loser buddies.

Maybe your spouse is increasingly distant and quiet.

Maybe your blood pressure is inching upward toward 140... 150... 160.

Maybe your "secure job" isn't so secure anymore.

Maybe you avoid answering the phone to avoid calls from creditors.

Maybe you avoid the stairs because you're out of breath after walking up just one flight.

The question is, what are you doing about the writing on your wall? Yes, it's easy to ignore or deny the writing. And yes, it takes a bit of courage to act. But resilient people act in the face of negative news. The sooner you act, the better chance you have of avoiding disaster.

Turn Adversity into Advantage

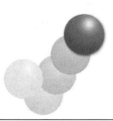

Turn Adversity into Advantage

Life is like a game of cards. The hand that is dealt you represents determinism; the way you play it is free will.

—Jawaharlal Nehru
1st prime minister of independent India

The character of Curious George would have been far less curious—and the books would have sold far fewer copies—if his creators, Margaret and H.A. Rey, hadn't narrowly escaped from the Nazis in 1940.

You see, in the early versions of *Curious George*, the monkey was much tamer and more of a loving, obedient pet. After their escape, the Reys projected their wartime experiences onto their fictional monkey, creating a mischievous character that's always on the run, narrowly avoiding disaster—escaping from jail, the zoo, the ocean, from atop a traffic light, from various angry mobs—only to return to the safety of home by the end of each adventure.

The Reys, like all resilient people, tapped into their personal experiences to turn *adversity into advantage*, which becomes Rule 2 of the *Top 10 Rules of Resilient People*.

Mining Childhood Miseries

Authors are notorious for mining their own experiences, no matter how unsavory, for material for their books. For many authors, writing is therapeutic. By writing about their miserable childhoods, they vent some of their shame and humiliation, which lingers for a lifetime.

Two of Charles Dickens' greatest novels, *Great Expectations* and *Oliver Twist*, for example, are reminiscent of Dickens' impoverished youth when he was forced to work 10 hours a day in a shoe polish factory while his father languished in debtors prison. A more recent example of an author turning childhood adversity into adult advantage is Frank McCourt, who won a Pulitzer Prize for *Angela's Ashes*, a heart-wrenching memoir of growing up impoverished in Ireland in the 1930s and '40s.

"It was, of course, a miserable childhood. The happy childhood is hardly worth your while," he often said with his dour Irish irony.

McCourt and Dickens are two of the millions of people who have turned adversity into advantage over the centuries. What qualities enable resilient people to bounce back when so many others in similar situations break under the weight of poverty, neglect, and disease?

FAST Your Way to Resiliency

Resilient people possess four key traits that empower them to turn lemons into lemonade. I use the acronym **FAST** to describe the traits that help people not just survive, but to thrive. Here's what each letter represents:

F – Face the facts

A – Attitude is everything

S – Seek solutions

T – Touch others

In this chapter, I'll use the original definition of the word *fast*: "firm; stable; secure," as in Langston Hughes' famous poem, "Hold *fast* to your dreams, for if dreams die, life is a broken-winged bird that cannot fly." Resilient people are FAST in their approach to dealing with pain; unlike most people who suppress pain, resilient people tap into pain and use it for material or motivation to achieve worthwhile goals.

In the chapter pages that follow, you'll read scores of real-life stories about people who turn adversity into advantage. All of these stories are inspiring, although more than a few were spawned from terrible tragedies.

Let's start our discussion with the first letter of FAST, which stands for *Face the facts*.

Face the Facts, No Matter How Painful

The first story involves TV and radio personality Leeza Gibbons and her crusade to assist caregivers of Alzheimer's patients. In 2000, Leeza's mother began her slow descent into what Leeza calls the "veil of Alzheimer's." While Leeza, her two siblings, and her father watched helplessly, she noted they all responded uniquely to their mother's mental decline:

"I saw my sister get depressed... my brother go into denial... and my father become isolated."

As a person in the public eye, Leeza had the leverage to effect positive change. Recognizing that the disease devastates the families and loved ones as well as the patient, Leeza chose to advocate on behalf of Alzheimer's *caregivers*, co-founding the Leeza Gibbons Memory Foundation to provide caregivers with resources and education for ensuring their own health and well-being. In eight centers across the country, caregivers are teamed with a "Leeza's Care Advocate" who helps them navigate the maze of issues that occur when a loved one is stricken.

Leeza was able to respond positively by way of her clinics because, unlike her father and siblings, *she faced the facts* that Alzheimer's "is not just about the person who has the disease but everyone who loves and cares for that person."

Facing ugly realities and dealing with them even applies to entire cultures and nations when it comes to turning adversity into advantage. A chilling example is present-day Rwanda in central Africa. Rwanda is dominated by two ethnic groups that have been warring for centuries, the majority Hutu and the minority Tutsi, who comprise only 15% of the population. In 1994, the long-bottled-up enmity broke loose, and the Hutu, led by militant militias, killed moderate Hutus and Tutsis at random, slaughtering nearly a million men, women, and children. In the 100-day bloodbath, nearly 20% of the population of Rwanda lost their lives.

After order was finally restored, President Paul Kagame enacted major changes to heal the divided country and end centuries of enmity between the Hutus and Tutsis. First, he ordered a genocide memorial to be erected atop a massive grave to remind the country of its failing. Then he set up "reconciliation villages," offering a free plot of land suitable for building a house to any family agreeing to live next to someone of the opposite ethnic group. Also, the government began paying women from different ethnic groups to sit in groups and weave "reconciliation baskets," which are sold all over the world; and every male of every ethnic group, from the richest to the poorest, must spend one Saturday a month cleaning the streets of the villages and cities.

"Hey, this happened to us, and it was horrible," said Kagame. "But we're going to tell the truth and face the truth, and the only way for it not to happen again is for us to let it go, to focus on what we have in common."

"Face the truth"—that's always step one for turning adversity into advantage.

Attitude Is Everything

The second key ingredient to overcoming adversity is Attitude. W. Clement Stone, a power-of-positive-thinking advocate and billionaire philanthropist, summed up the importance of attitude this way:

"There is little difference in people—but that little difference makes a big difference. The little difference is attitude. The big difference is whether it is positive or negative."

When Olympic champion figure skater Scott Hamilton was diagnosed with cancer, he fought the disease with the same determination that helped him win a gold medal in the 1984 Olympics. Hamilton feels we're defined by how we deal with setbacks, and one way he has dealt with cancer is to raise $10 million for research and cancer awareness. He's living proof of the power of a positive attitude.

"The only true disability in life is a bad attitude," says Hamilton.

American inventor Thomas Edison epitomized a person with a great attitude. When a fire burned his laboratory to the ground, Edison comforted his research assistants with these words: "Friends, there is great value in disaster. Look at these ashes—all of our mistakes have burned up! Thank God we can start anew."

Keeping a positive attitude after losing a laboratory in a fire would be tough enough, but remaining positive after losing a spouse to assassins during a political campaign would be nearly impossible. But Corazon Aquino did just that after her husband was murdered as he prepared to run for election against corrupt Philippine President Fernando Marcos. Pressed by supporters to run in her husband's place, the shy Aquino, who called herself a "plain housewife," reluctantly agreed to take her husband's place against the might Marcos.

Her confidence grew as her popularity increased, and when Marcos declared himself the winner of the rigged election, Aquino bravely led a nationwide protest that overthrew Marcos and made her president in 1986. She used her seven years in office to reform the government, limit the power of the presidency, and restore democracy to the Philippines.

"Nothing can stop the man [or woman] with the right mental attitude," said Thomas Jefferson. "Nothing on earth can help the man with the wrong attitude."

Seek Solutions

The third letter in the FAST approach to turning adversity into advantage is "S" for *Seek solutions*. In the book *Your Brain at Work*, the author cites research that proves the brain works differently for people who focus on solutions versus people who focus on problems. People who ruminate over problems activate parts of the brain that signal avoidance. Their bodies stiffen and their minds get stuck in neutral.

When people *seek solutions*, on the other hand, the creative right hemisphere of the brain becomes activated, producing an action orientation, which primes the brain for insight. In short, the mental process of focusing on problems *freezes* our brains—so no plans of attack can be hatched—while the process of focusing on solutions *frees* our brains so that solutions can be cooked up and acted on. (The word "brainstorming" accurately describes the action-oriented mental process that takes place when we seek solutions.)

Entrepreneurs understand the importance of seeking solutions. Instead of complaining about problems… or avoiding problems… entrepreneurs see problems as opportunities in work clothes, and they recognize that the bigger the problem, the bigger the opportunity.

As a freshman at Southern Methodist University, Blake Mycoskie spotted a problem in his dorm that plagued most young men and women on their own for the first time—piles of dirty clothing stacked up in their rooms, sometimes sitting unwashed for weeks. So, Blake started his first venture, a door-to-door laundry business for students at SMU. After expanding the business to four colleges, he sold EZ Laundry and moved to Nashville.

During a trip to Argentina on vacation, he saw hundreds of shoeless children who were suffering from cuts and infections to their feet. To complicate matters, barefoot children weren't allowed to attend school, effectively limiting them to a life of poverty.

Instead of donating used shoes to poor families, as many well-to-do and well-meaning Argentines were doing, Blake sought a more seamless solution:

"And then it hit me," he said. "Instead of starting a charity with handouts, why not create a company where charity is the whole purpose. I thought, 'I'll get people to buy one pair of shoes today so we can give away one pair tomorrow. We'll call them Tomorrow Shoes. No, we'll call them Tom's Shoes for tomorrow.'"

In 2006, Mycoskie started manufacturing *alpargatas*, the Spanish name for rubber-soled shoes with canvas uppers. According to *The Wall Street Journal*, in the four years since its founding, Tom's Shoes has given away 600,000 shoes while racking up $33 million in sales.

That's what is known as a "win-win" in any language.

Touching, and Teaching, Others

The final letter of the FAST acronym stands for *Touch others*. In researching this book, I've noticed that one trait of resilient people is their desire to share their ability to bounce with others. Most resilient people recognize that they're not alone in their struggle to bounce back from adversity, and they often set up support groups, organizations, or corporations to share their stories and strategies with others.

Eunice Kennedy Shriver is a great example of someone who touched tens of thousands, if not millions, of lives with an organization that truly turned adversity into advantage. Shriver grew up with a mentally challenged sister, Rosemary, who was left permanently incapacitated by a lobotomy at age 23. In 1968, inspired by her sister's challenges, Shriver co-founded the Special Olympics to allow mentally and physically challenged adults to participate in Olympic-type competitions. The official credo of the Special Olympics, which has now spread to 170 countries, could serve as a mission statement for every person who is fighting an uphill battle in their lives:

Let me win. But if I cannot win, let me be brave in the attempt.

The Special Olympics credo could have been written to describe Shannon Horne, who knows something about bravery and winning: She's jumped out of an airplane, and she's a regular participant in horseback riding, rowing, and surfing despite being confined to a wheelchair due to cerebral palsy. Oh, and if that's not enough, this 28-year-old mother of two was crowned 2010 Ms. Wheelchair Florida at a pageant in Tampa. An advocate for disabled Americans, Horne also does volunteer work and is developing an East Coast team of dancers for a group in California that works with dancers who are disabled.

The third example of touching others dealing with adversity was retold in the stirring movie *Extraordinary Measures*, starring Harrison Ford, seen by millions of viewers around the globe. The movie chronicles the challenge that John Crowley and his family faced when his two young children were diagnosed with Pompe disease, a fatal degenerative disease.

Refusing to accept his children's death sentence, Crowley quit his job with pharmaceutical giant Bristol-Myers Squibb and invested his life savings in a biotech startup to discover treatments for the disease.

"We were originally told they wouldn't live to be 2, and then maybe 5 or 10. Thanks to the medicine we helped develop, Megan just turned 13 and Patrick is turning 12. They're our little miracles."

The medicine reversed the life-threatening enlargement of their hearts, but Pompe is a neuromuscular disease that affects not just skeletal muscle but breathing and cardiac muscles, so the parents measure their children's lives in moments and months, instead of years.

The bright side to this tragic story is that Crowley's startup company has been acquired by Genzyme, the world's third-largest bio-technology company. Newer and better medicines developed at Genzyme keep extending Megan and Patrick's lives and offer hope for children stricken with Pompe and other rare genetic diseases in the future.

Compared to What?

When you read stories like the ones in this chapter, it's hard for most of us dealing with daily nuisances, or even major setbacks, for that matter, to feel sorry for ourselves. Let's face it, the prospect of losing your home to the bank—a devastating reality for thousands of Americans—doesn't even compare to losing a child.

Not even close.

Resilient people know this, and they maintain an attitude of gratitude, even in the darkest hours, because they understand that no matter how much adversity they're facing in their lives, there is always someone who has it much worse… yet is dealing nobly with their disasters.

In the next chapter, *Resilient Rule 3: Put Things into Perspective*, we're going to look at some people who were dealt very bad hands in life but are playing them brilliantly.

As Shannon Horne, Ms. Wheelchair Florida, put it, "I do not believe in crying about how my life is different from what is considered the norm. You only get one life, and every day I live mine to the best of my ability."

So should we all.

Put Things into Perspective

Put Things into Perspective

*The real discovery consists not in seeking new
landscapes but in having new eyes.*

—Marcel Proust

Tim Kimball's neighbors owe him an apology.

They reported Tim to their local homeowners' association because his yard became overgrown. They assumed he was lazy.

They were wrong. Tim is anything but lazy.

In fact, Tim would not only *love* to mow his own lawn, he'd happily mow their lawn *for free* if he could.

But he can't.

Tim is a quadriplegic who can't move his body below his neck.

Perspective Changed with a Punch

When Tim was 20, his life changed in a flash. He was at a club during a break from college when some drunk guys pushed through the crowd. Tim refused to step aside. He got slugged in the face and fell awkwardly, hitting his head on a metal box and dislocating his neck.

"I remember trying to get up, and I couldn't move. That's pretty much it."

Tim was living with his mother for a year after the accident when she pushed him to go back to school. He reluctantly agreed and was astonished to discover how much easier college had become.

"I didn't have the same distractions that I had before. It was easier to focus. I didn't have much else to do, so I did my schoolwork."

Tim learned to operate his computer with a mouthstick and voice recognition software. Today he is nearing completion of an architectural program and plans to work in a small design firm or start his own business.

The Importance of Putting Things into Perspective

Tim's resilience is helping him cope, but he still misses the everyday things most of us take for granted. Like mowing the lawn. Scratching his nose when it itches. Tearing the cellophane off a pack of crackers. And feeling the shower on his face.

I tell you Tim's story to illustrate the importance of putting things into perspective. From Tim's perspective, mowing the lawn becomes a pleasure, instead of a pain, doesn't it? The tedious things so many people gripe about—taking out the garbage... cleaning the house... washing the car... commuting to and from work—Tim would *pay* to do. If only he could.

One of my biggest pet peeves is people who make mountains out of molehills... people whose perspectives stop at the end of their noses. Some people act as if the world is supposed to stop spinning when they break a fingernail.

Any time you're having a bad day, here's a simple question to ask yourself to put things into perspective:

Compared to what?

Let's say the water heater goes on the blink, and there's no hot water for morning showers. Is this is a crisis? *Compared to what?* Compared to the *4 billion* people around the globe who lack indoor plumbing, a cold sponge bath once in a blue moon is a minor *inconvenience*, but not a *crisis*. Resilient people put things into perspective, equipping them to recognize the difference between a crisis and an inconvenience.

To my way of thinking, inconveniences are good for us because they offer us opportunities to practice bouncing. Think of inconveniences as dress rehearsals for the *real* crises we have to face in life. By learning to roll with the punches when the unexpected smacks us in the face, we're less likely to break when a real crisis hits—and rest assured, there's a crisis waiting in the wings for all of us.

If THEY Can Do It, YOU Can Do It

Speaking of a crisis, America is facing a *national crisis*—obesity. According to the American Medical Association, nearly 66% of adults in the U.S. are classified as obese (and sadly, the rest of the industrialized world is following our lead). All the experts agree that one of the basics to controlling weight is to walk 30 minutes a day.

Walking—it's easy. It's natural. It's good for the body and the soul. Yet fewer than 2 out of 10 adults regularly exercise by walking or running.

Hey, I've heard all the excuses. I've USED all the excuses from time to time: "I'm too tired in the morning; I'm too tired after work; I'm on my feet all day; I don't have anyone to walk with me." Yada, yada, yada.

Those are all valid excuses, right?

Compared to what?

Compared to Robyn Stawski, those excuses are wa-a-a-y lame. Robyn Stawski's excuses for not walking would knock your excuses into next Tuesday… yet, walk she does, each and every day.

You see, Robyn was born with cerebral palsy, making her muscles and joints rigid and inflexible. Her condition was so severe she was confined to a wheelchair through eighth grade. For her, walking is anything but natural. It's a painful chore. Yet, in 2009, the 32-year-old Robyn set a goal of walking an entire mile without the aid of arm crutches. For Robyn, it was a brutal, bruising goal. Every 10 seconds or so her legs would give out, and she'd fall to her knees.

"A light pole. Just make it to the light pole," she'd plead with herself. "After that, the sign ahead. Get up and make it to the sign."

Her first unassisted mile walk took one hour and 43 minutes.

Four months later, she set a personal best of 24 minutes.

Compared to Robyn, being too tired to walk isn't much of an excuse, is it?

Personal Best Is Best

Robyn Stawski's personal best time in the mile is more than 20 minutes slower than the world record. But resilient people like Robyn understand that *personal bests*—not world record bests—are the ultimate measure of achievement. We're not all blessed with Olympic talent, but we *are* all blessed with Olympian resilience if we choose to draw on it.

Chris Broyles is another victim of cerebral palsy who refuses to let his physical limitations hold him back. As a junior in high school, Broyles joined the cross-country team. His personal best was a sluggish 10 minutes a mile. After his first season, Chris set a goal of running a mile in six minutes. He ran all summer and into the fall, and by the end of his final year in cross-country, he got within eight seconds of his goal.

"I think he started out being an inspiration to us," said his coach, Chris Biernacki. "Now, he's just one of the guys, and I think that's the best part of it. They treat him as one of their own brothers out there."

"My coach taught me not to let your limitations put you down," Chris says.

Do Something Different

Chris and Robyn have made great strides despite their physical limitations through perseverance and determination. But just think of the millions of people who let their *mental limitations* hold them back from accomplishing personal bests.

That's why it's crucial to do something different in your life... to challenge your limitations... to park your excuses at the curb, lace up your running shoes (or lace up your courage) and head in a different direction. You may find yourself accomplishing more than you ever dreamed possible.

Maybe you'd love to start a new business... learn a new trade... change career paths... retire early... invest in the stock market... grow roses... get a college degree... remodel a house... restore an antique automobile—whatever your dormant dreams are, you can achieve them if you commit yourself to doing something different.

Now, I know what many of you are thinking: *"Sure, I'd love to start my own business... or invest in the stock market... or go back to school, but what if I fail? There's risk involved in trying something new, so I'm better off just doing what I've always been doing."*

Hey, no one wants to fail. Reducing risk is a legitimate concern. Notice I said "reducing risk," not *eliminating* risk. Some risk is unavoidable in life, for *not* to risk is to risk. In other words, sometimes doing the same old thing is riskier than doing something new. Think of the 2 million-plus people in the U.S. alone, plus the tens of millions more globally, who "played it safe" and still lost their jobs in the latest recession. They might have delayed opening a business because the economic climate was "too risky," only to find out days later they had been laid off from what they thought was a "safe, secure job."

So much for job security.

Evaluating a Risk

This is a good time to talk about the role that resilience plays in risk taking. As I said, you can't *eliminate* risk, for, to paraphrase Robert Burns, "The best-laid plans of mice and men often go awry"—but you can *reduce* risk.

Years ago I heard an interview with Norman Lear, creator of the '70s hit TV show, *All in the Family*. The interviewer asked Lear how he evaluated risk.

Lear replied that he always asks himself two questions before jumping into a new project. *"What is the worst that can happen? And if the worst happens, can I live with it?"*

Personally, I've asked myself those two questions dozens of times over the years when I was on the brink of making a big decision in my life. I asked myself those two questions before I resigned from teaching and moved to Tampa, Florida, in 1986 to open a training business. I had no job lined up, didn't know anyone other than my parents, who lived 45 minutes away, and only had $20,000 in the bank to tide me over until my business took off.

What's the worst that could happen? I could burn through my money and fall on my face in business.

Could I live with it? I figured if that happened, I'd move in with my parents for a few weeks until I found a job, so, yes, I could live with it.

I took the risk, and it was one of the best decisions I ever made. Today I operate two profitable businesses out of my home—a publishing company and a real estate investment company. I've got a great wife… three great kids… and a smart, handsome, rock-'em, sock-'em grandson. I live in a lakefront home that's paid for, own five rental properties, have zero debt, and manage half a million dollars in retirement accounts.

All because I took a calculated risk 25 years ago. .

Hey, not all my risks have worked out. I've been fired twice, had to close three businesses, lost a few thousand on a bad loan to a friend, and have written a couple of books that barely sold enough copies to cover the printing cost.

But those were failures *I could live with*, and I was well aware of that going into the deals. Yeah, I failed, but the failures weren't devastating. In fact, the lessons I learned equipped me to make better decisions in the future, so I actually benefited from those failures.

Putting Risk into Perspective

The risks I've taken in my life, and likely the ones you've taken, are teeny-tiny compared to some of the giant risks people have taken that changed the course of history.

When Columbus set sail in three small, leaky boats to look for a new route to India... *that* was a huge risk. Same goes for Magellan when he commanded the first expedition to sail around the globe.

When millions of immigrants from Europe and Asia paid their last pennies to sail shoulder to shoulder in steerage for weeks across violent seas with the hope of gaining freedom and opportunity... *that* was a huge risk.

When Eisenhower gave the command for allied forces to attack German troops by invading Normandy beaches with 150,000 troops, nearly 7,000 watercraft, accompanied by 1,200 airplanes—now, *that* was a huge risk. (Eisenhower even penned a letter taking full responsibility in the event the allied effort failed.)

I could give a thousand other examples of monumental risks that paid huge dividends when they succeeded... or led to huge disasters when they failed (Napoleon's defeat at Waterloo comes quickly to mind).

When you put your risks into a historical perspective, they don't seem so life altering, do they? When you compare taking a calculated risk to start a business... or change careers... or follow a dream, you're not putting your life on the line. And I certainly wouldn't suggest you court financial disaster by mortgaging your house to buy a franchise unless you have a viable Plan B and Plan C in case the worst happens.

Remember… if the worst happens and you *cannot* live with it, then don't do it. But the corollary is this: Nothing ventured, nothing gained.

I'll leave you with an anonymous poem about a cautious fellow who was so fearful of failure that he never took a risk in life. I hope it inspires you to rekindle your dreams:

There was a very cautious man

Who never laughed or played.

He never risked, he never tried;

He never sang or prayed.

And when he one day passed away

His insurance was denied.

For since he never lived,

They claimed he never died.

Make Your Own Movie

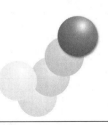

Make Your Own Movie

All men should strive to learn, before they die,
What they are running from, and to, and why.
—James Thurber
author & cartoonist

"You're at a lucky place in your life," the admissions officer said to my daughter, Sydney. "At our school, you get to write your own script and make your own movie."

Sydney nodded and faked a smile.

"I like that," I said to the woman as I jotted down her comment on the front cover of my orientation booklet. "Make your own movie. I like that."

We were enrolling Sydney at a boarding school in Utah for her senior year in high school. All Sydney could think of was how to get a cell phone so she could call her friends back in Florida to tell them how horrible her parents were and how miserable she was going to be for the next 12 months.

All I could think about was how much she would grow at Oakley during her senior year. And grow, she did. She learned how to snowboard, made new friends, made great grades, worked on the yearbook staff, got accepted into college, and, best of all, broke ties with a few nasty, negative kids that were leading her down a dark alley back home in Tampa.

Her "movie" is still not finished, of course. It's a lifetime project. But the plot has taken a happier, healthier twist since her days at Oakley.

Don't Let Others Define You

"Life isn't about finding yourself. Life is about creating yourself," quipped Irish author George Bernard Shaw. The movie-musical version of Shaw's most famous play, *My Fair Lady*, revolves around the theme of self-creation. In the movie, Professor Higgins, a cold, snobby linguist, "creates" a charming lady from Eliza Doolittle, a lower class and unschooled flower girl. By the end of the movie, the professor has fallen in love with his "creation," but she rejects him because he fails to give her the proper credit for her transformation.

In a sense, we're all a lot like Eliza Doolittle. People enter our lives, often by chance, with the intention of creating us in their image. They can charm us or persuade us or even bully us. But in the end, we create ourselves by *choosing* to accept or reject the influence of others.

Where we get in trouble is when we turn our back on our true selves and let others define us. When we give more weight to external beliefs than our own internal ones, then we run the risk of losing our way. "To your own self be true," said Shakespeare. "But if you don't know who your self is, then you run the risk of *being true to someone else's values and beliefs*.

Totalitarian nations gain their power to rule by empowering the state to define individuals, and when individuals buy into the state's propaganda, the result is North Korea, which is based on a cult of personality of the founder, the late Kim Il Sung, and his dictator son, Kim Jong Il. Portraits and statues of the father and son adorn every building and street corner in every city in North Korea. Dear Leader worship is so ingrained in the culture that political prisoners facing a firing squad will often shout, "Long Live Kim!" seconds before soldiers fire their leveled rifles.

No Self, No Resilience

It boggles my mind that anyone could be so loyal to a political cause that they'd praise the regime that orders their death. But that's what can happen when people allow someone else to define them.

In all fairness to the North Korean people, they couldn't make their own movie even if they wanted. The communist-run regime controls the media... controls the schools... controls the economy... controls the police... controls the military, and, thus, controls the people. It's impossible to march to a different drummer when the government owns the drums and dictates which rhythms can be played. Fortunately, North Korea is the exception and not the rule. People who live in democracies are free, for the most part, to script their own lives.

Fighting Rejection Infection

You can't bounce back from adversity if your self worth is yoked to other people's opinions of you. Rejection is like an infection—it can't hurt you unless it enters your body. Resilient people build up immunities to rejection, and many times they turn others' negative assessments into opportunities.

Truth is, even the most successful people experience rejection from time to time, but they understand that rejection is a speed bump, not a stop sign, and they treat rejection as a challenge to overcome rather than a permanent reversal of fortune.

Warren Buffett, the most successful investor of the 20th century, was rejected by Harvard Business School after graduating from the University of Nebraska. "This was a crushing event at the time, but everything I thought was a crushing event at the time has turned out for the better."

After Harvard rejected him, Buffett researched other opportunities and discovered that two investing experts he admired, Benjamin Graham and David Dodd, were teaching at Columbia's graduate business school. Columbia accepted Buffett, and from these two mentors he learned the core principles that have guided his investing philosophy for more than 50 years. Oh, ironically, Harvard's loss was Columbia's gain, as Buffett donated more than $12 million to Columbia in 2008.

Buffett has a lot of company in the long list of people who were rejected by Ivy League schools but went on to forge successful careers in business, journalism, and medicine. *Today* show host Meredith Vieira was also devastated by being rejected by the school of her dreams—once again, Harvard—but it turned out to be a blessing in disguise, as it was a mentor at Tufts University who sparked Vieira's interest in journalism by offering her an internship. "Had I not been rejected," she says, "I doubt I would have entered the field."

Harvard has a long tradition of rejecting resilient people who bounce back from the negative experience and move on to stellar careers. Dr. Harold Varmus was rejected not once, but twice, from Harvard. One Harvard interviewer criticized him for being "inconsistent and immature" and advised him to enlist in the military. Once more, Harvard's rejection turned out to be Columbia's rejoicing, as Dr. Varmus went on to win the Nobel Prize in medicine and is now the president of Memorial Sloan-Kettering Cancer Center in New York.

Yet another Harvard reject, Columbia president Lee Bollinger, sums up the importance of developing a strong sense of self to shield yourself from rejection: "Don't let rejections control your life," he says. "It's a big mistake to let other people's assessments of you determine your own self assessment. The question really is, 'At the end of the day, who is going to make the determination about what your talents are and what your interests are?' That has to be you."

Resilience Leads to Reinvention

You must be resilient to make your own movie, and that means having the confidence to sort through other people's opinions—accepting constructive criticism when it makes you a better director of your life, while ignoring criticism that is unwarranted and wide of the mark. Resilience may also require you to rewrite your script when interesting new characters enter your movie or when unforeseen circumstances force you to change your plot. In that case, resilience may require you to *reinvent yourself* by recasting yourself in a different form.

Today, with seismic changes happening in days and months instead of decades, the job you're good at may not exist tomorrow, so to survive, you must be willing to reinvent yourself to stay ahead of the curve. Only 25 years ago, you could have been the best carburetor repairman... or the best typewriter repairman... or the best stereo repairman in the city, and you could go to sleep at night knowing you'd always have steady employment.

Today, you'd be out of a job.

Fifteen years ago I wrote in a book that, according to the U.S. Labor Bureau, the average worker in the U.S. will have 10 to 12 different jobs in four to five different career areas during their working lifetime. And I wrote that statement *before* the Internet kicked into high gear... before smart phones... before China gobbled up most of our manufacturing... before the worst recession since the Great Depression.

Today, change is happening at warp speed, which means reinvention isn't a luxury anymore. It's a necessity.

Imagine, for example, that in 2005 you were the regional manager for a dozen Blockbuster stores in a major metropolitan area. You've got a great salary and own a ton of company stock. Then along comes an online video rental site called Netflix, followed by a vending machine video rental outfit called Redbox. In three years, low-cost competition forces you to close six of your stores, and in three more years, Blockbuster will likely be bankrupt, and you'll likely be looking for work.

Reinvention—these days it's the rule, not the exception.

So get used to it and get good at it.

Take a Tip from Big Pharma

To learn how reinvention works, we need only take a lesson from, of all places, giant pharmaceutical companies, which, out of necessity, have decades of experience in reinventing their products.

Here's why:

When Big Pharma invents a new drug, they can charge pretty much what they want for it, which means a high-demand drug becomes a money machine for the lucky manufacturer. For example, Lipitor, the bestselling drug in the U.S., sells for around $150 for a 30-day supply at your local pharmacy. Pfizer earns *$10 billion a year* off this one cholesterol-lowering drug.

One catch. By law, brand-name drugs lose their patents after 12 years, and because Lipitor is scheduled to go off patent soon, it will be available in much-cheaper generic form, causing Pfizer's revenue, and stock price, to drop like a brick.

But Big Pharma has come up with a way to "reinvent" their top-selling drugs. Right before a drug is ready to come off patent, the company announces it has "reformulated" the drug. That way they can claim a new invention… and extend the patent another 12 years. Pharmaceutical companies discovered that the simplest way to reformulate a drug was to apply a special coating to make it longer-lasting, and—bam!—there it is, the same old drug in a "new, improved" form at the same high price as the original. That's why you'll see the letters "XL" after so many big-selling brand-name drugs—XL stands for "extended release," and all a manufacturer had to do was recoat the original formulation and keep counting the cash.

The patent-extension strategy is a favorite way for Big Pharma to indefinitely delay their patent expiration dates and thwart their generic competitors. The practice has become so widespread that it's even got a name—*evergreening.*

Evergreen Yourself

Evergreening offers an obvious parallel to our lives.

In the workplace, you're like a product—a formulated drug, if you will. Your formula is made up of a mixture of skills that employers or your clients pay you for. Most of your *general skills*—promptness, communicating effectively, organizing your work, etc.—are transferable from one job to another... from one career to another... or, if need be, from employment to self-employment.

Think of these general skills that you've spent a lifetime cultivating as your *basic formulation* and the new specific skills as your *special coating*. Once you blend your new skills with the old ones—you've reinvented yourself... you're *evergreened*!

If you've been a good teacher or engineer or manager, for example, you've had to lead people, persuade them, motivate them, set goals, build teams, meet deadlines... and on and on. No matter what your career, you still have to do all those things. Before you can sell anything, you have to sell yourself first, right? If you can sell insurance, you have to sell trust and confidence before you can sell a client car insurance. If you can teach literature to high school students, as I did, then you can teach personal growth principles to adults, which is what I'm doing right now.

I'm proof that evergreening is possible. I've done a dozen different things since I was 40 years old, and the skills I've drawn on the most in each of those positions was my basic formulation—my general skills. To paraphrase Robert Fulghum's wise book, "All I really need to know I learned teaching high school English."

I've always been able to write reasonably well, but in order to reinvent myself as a publisher, I had to learn some specific skills: Learning about layouts... cover art... printing requirements... copyright laws... managing inventory and shipping—that sort of thing. There was a learning curve, of course, but 90% of my efforts involve general skills I've drawn on since college: researching... planning my workdays...

organizing material... coordinating projects... communicating with team members... follow up—those types of tasks. Unless you need *highly specific skills* in your career—like becoming a surgeon or dentist or CPA—then reinventing yourself is easier than you think.

Beware the Negative Naysayers

The biggest obstacle to reinventing yourself isn't your skill set—it's your peer set, your so-called friends and acquaintances. For every supportive friend, you'll have 10 friends that will try to dash your dreams. Hugh MacLeod, author of *Ignore Everybody and 39 Other Keys to Creativity*, thinks he knows why:

"People like you the way you are. They are used to interacting with you in a certain way and don't want you to change. Your decision to change yourself or change careers may threaten their world view."

In effect, naysayers are more concerned about getting left behind than they are about your failing. If you grow... if you reinvent yourself... if you change and they don't, it reminds them of their own dashed dreams. For every person who has the courage to change the plotline in their own movie, there are countless others who stay in dissatisfying jobs because they listen too closely to people telling them not to make the leap.

Well, I'm here to tell you I made the leap from the safe, secure job of teaching to opening my own business. It was the best decision I ever made. Let's turn to the next chapter to see why the best part in the movie of your life is the scene called, "Be Your Own Boss."

That scene is sure to win you an Oscar.

Be the Boss of 'Me'

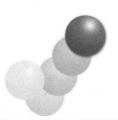

Be the Boss of 'Me'

*The multitude have no habit of self reliance
or original action. The best lightning rod
for your protection is your own spine.*
—Ralph Waldo Emerson
On Self-Reliance

I watched as 5-year-old David sat in his older brother's lap, alternately *pulling* his big brother Don closer... and then *pushing* him away. When Don would calmly ask David to sit still, the younger brother's response was always the same.

"You are not the boss of me."

This routine went on for a full five minutes, always accompanied by the same response when Don entreated David to sit still or move to another chair.

"You are not the boss of me."

Driving home, I shook my head thinking of David's display and muttered to myself, "Kids, they don't know what they want." Then it suddenly occurred to me—we've all got some David in us, whether we're 5... or 25... or 55... or 85... makes no difference. All our lives we send mixed messages to authority figures. We pull them closer... and then push them away. Pull them closer... then push them away, all the while chanting to ourselves:

"You are not the boss of me."

Mixed Messages

Most people sabotage their progress in life because of their habit of pulling and pushing their way through life, saying one thing while doing the opposite.

Most people say they don't like their jobs, for example—according to *Forbes* magazine, nearly 90% of Americans are unhappy with work—yet few make an effort to open their own business.

Most people *say* they want a secure, worry-free retirement, yet they don't save and invest, which is why for 50% of Americans age 62 or older, Social Security is their sole source of income.

Most people *say* they want the federal government to spend less and "stay out of their lives," yet they keep cashing their checks from a long list of entitlement programs.

We're sending mixed messages to our government, our children, and ourselves when we pull forward and push away at the same time. I saw a great example of this pull/push phenomenon during a TV segment on the modern-day Tea Party movement, which touts itself as wanting something most sane, sensible Americans support—less government spending and interference in our lives.

When a reporter asked a white-haired, grandmotherly-looking Tea Party participant what she wanted the movement to accomplish, she replied straight-faced, "I want the government to keep its hands off my Medicare." The fact that the federal government funds and runs Medicare was lost on the woman.

I'm not knocking the Tea Party-ers. I'm all for smaller government, less federal spending and less debt. But when someone says they're against big government while they're picking Uncle Sam's pockets, well, they're not just kidding themselves, they're acting like a kid, pulling and pushing on the same person at the same time.

Time to act like grownups, don't you think?

What It Means to 'Be the Boss of Me'

Grownups understand that Being the Boss of Me drills down to self-reliance. Self-reliance—that's the bedrock that supports everything else in the lives of healthy, productive people. Self-reliant people are more resilient than dependent people for the same reason that mature adults are more resilient than spoiled children. To be truly self-reliant, you need to follow certain codes of behavior.

I've identified 10 rules that self-reliant people follow, enabling them to take control and be the boss of their own lives. Here are the 10 rules for building resilience through self-reliance.

10 Rules to Follow to Become the Boss of Me

1. *Set goals:* "If you don't know where you're going, any road will take you there," wrote Lewis Carroll in *Alice in Wonderland.* So true, which is why so many people float through life like a feather on a spring breeze, until they wake up one day and say, "Hey, I'm 60 and sick and broke and friendless. What happened?" Being the Boss of Me means setting your own course, rather than going through life like you're on a scavenger hunt, following someone else's directions and adhering to their goals until the game of life ends. Goals give you direction and purpose and a feeling of accomplishment when they're achieved. Experts suggest you break goals down into long-term, medium-term, and short-term goals and write them down, although, frankly, I seldom do. Personally, I choose to tell my goals to my friends or my wife, which motivates me to achieve my goals or be forced to lose face, which I hate to do. Whether written or spoken or mental, the bottom line is that resilient people set goals and keep working until they accomplish them or replace them with revised goals.

2. *Set deadlines:* When I tell people I write books, about half the time someone will say, "Oh, I've always wanted to write a book"… or "I started a book but didn't finish it." Simple truth—unless they set a deadline, they never will finish their book. I was motivated to start writing by a friend who said to me, "Never die with a book in you." That comment hit me like a punch in the nose. I had talked about writing a book for years but never got around to it. The thought of me lying on my deathbed regretting that I never had the discipline to accomplish my greatest aspiration overwhelmed me, so the next day, I got to work. Deciding what to write about and committing to it was the first step. But I knew from writing my doctoral dissertation that without a deadline, good intentions can disappear like smoke up a chimney, so I set realistic deadlines of writing one chapter a week for 10 weeks. Sure enough, at the end of 2 1/2 months, I had a manuscript ready for the printer. Since the first book, I've authored or co-written 20 books. And they all began just as the book you're holding began—with a title and a deadline.

3. Set your schedule: I'm sure you're heard the platitude, "Plan your work and work your plan." That's what people who are the Boss of Me do—they set schedules and stick to them. Ever watch one of those live-from-prison *Lockup* documentaries on MSNBC? The more violent and pathological the prisoners are, the more structured their days are. The worst offenders are allowed out of their cells only one hour a day. The rest of the time they're locked in solitary confinement. Why? Because they're incapable of scheduling their days productively, so prison has to schedule it for them. The corollary holds true also: The better you become at scheduling your day and accomplishing your goals, the freer you are.

4. Start projects: I have an overweight, out-of-shape friend who jokes that she goes to the YWCA once every year—to renew her annual membership. She doesn't stay to use the equipment. She just stays long enough to drop off her check and get her photo taken for her renewed membership card. It's become an annual ritual—she's been doing this for five years. Yet she's never started an exercise program. Why? She's afraid if she starts, she might feel obligated to use the facility regularly, which she doesn't want to do because she hates to exercise. So she gets heavier each year... and her knees hurt more each year... and her blood pressure goes up each year. And it will continue to do so as long as she refuses to START an exercise program. People don't *start* exercising... or *start* dieting... or *start* new businesses for the same reason I was reluctant to *start writing books*—the project seems overwhelming. But I learned from writing my first book that I don't write books, I write four to five hours a day, five days a week, for 10 weeks, and at the end of 10 weeks, *a book magically appears.* Same goes for dieting and fitness. You don't lose 50 pounds—you adjust your daily eating and exercise routines and discover that you can easily drop a pound a day. Then, after two months, you discover that you've lost 50 pounds! But first you gotta START YOUR PROJECT!

5. Finish what you start: A former business partner of mine was great at starting things—businesses, books, training programs, remodeling projects. You name it, he could start it. He started 16 different companies in the 15 years I worked with him. Only two made money. The rest just sat there, corporations without any staff... without any funding... without any products... without any sales. Each of the companies looked promising at the start. They started with a purpose, a business plan, a direction, and a schedule. But somewhere along the way, my ex-partner would lose interest. He'd abandon working on one project to start another one... then another one... and another, never finishing what he started. He's always hustling to keep his head above water. Not hard to figure out why, is it?

6. *Seek professional advice (but decide for yourself):* You can't be the Boss of Me if you don't know what you're doing, so you have to acquire some specialized knowledge in your fields of endeavor. For example, I've bought and renovated dozens of townhouses and condos over the last 30 years, so

I've learned enough about construction to direct construction projects. And I always, ALWAYS ask contractors and workers their opinions on what to do and how to do it. And contractors *love* giving their opinions. But I've learned that when a contractor says something can't be done, it usually means he doesn't want to do it. So, I've learned to ask their opinion *("If it were your house, Mr. Contractor, what would you do?")*... to listen with an open mind... and then to make the decision myself. I once hired an interior decorator at $500 an hour to make design suggestions for my home in Tampa. She was professional. She was knowledgeable. She was creative. She made two pages of suggestions for design alterations. I didn't take a single one. My house is a hodgepodge of styles—contemporary, mid-century, African, pop art, Japanese woodblock prints, and a dozen handmade quilts. I even use an abandoned table from a high school biology lab for my office worktable. My wife and I love our eclectic furnishings and art, and in the end, that's really all that counts.

7. *Create multiple streams of income:* Nearly 15 million people lost their jobs—and for most, their only source of income—during the recession of 2007 to 2009, and, as a result, foreclosures and bankruptcies skyrocketed. People with jobs can't really be the Boss of Me unless they have significant savings to fall back on or multiple sources of income. Unfortunately, few Americans have either, making them especially vulnerable during economic downturns. It's tough to be resilient when your only source of income suddenly dries up. Here's how to protect yourself in the future: 1) Start a side business working evenings and weekends while you still have a job; in the event you lose your job, it will be easier to ratchet up your part-time work into a full-time career. 2) Pay yourself first by depositing at least 20% of your income into an automatic withdrawal savings account; 3) Take full advantage of any 401(k) plans offered by your employer, especially if they match contributions; 4) Make the maximum contribution to a Roth IRA every year—your money is taxed when it goes in but withdrawals are tax free— and it's a good bet taxes will be going up, up, up in the years ahead; 5) Learn about investing in stocks, bonds, and income-producing instruments. A good place to start is to subscribe to *The Chartist* mutual fund/ETF letter. The fund invests in only 15 ETFs and has averaged a compounded gain of 11.89% for nearly 25 years, which means for $250 a year, you can get returns equal to the top 5% of money managers.

8. *Put your health first:* A recent study of 5,000 British adults over a 20-year period revealed that four common bad habits combined—smoking cigarettes, drinking too much alcohol, lack of exercise, and a poor diet—can age you 12 years! Of the participants in the study who had all four bad habits, nearly one out of three died during the 20 years of the study. Among the participants without any of the bad habits, only 8% died during the study. Think of it this way—your health doesn't affect just you. It affects your spouse… your children… your friends… your co-workers. Unless you're a real louse, your friends and family want you to live a long, healthy, prosperous life. If your being overweight and out of shape contributes to your getting Type II diabetes… or a heart attack… or a stroke, then your illness can impact dozens of people. If you're not motivated to improve your health for yourself, do it for those who care about you.

9. *Take regular inventory:* Businesses take inventory at least once a year, sometimes quarterly, to keep track of products in stock so they can track profits and better serve their customers. To Be the Boss of Me, you need to take inventory of your life—all areas of your life—to keep track of your personal profit and loss performance. Here's how to begin: Break your life down into five categories, the Five *Fs*, I call them: faith… family… friends… finances… and fitness. I even add a sixth F that I consider vitally important to Being the Boss of Me— Freedom. At least twice a year, sit down with your spouse and check on the status of each of these categories. If you find yourself slipping in an area, set a goal to get back on track. It's a lot easier to deal with your credit card debt when it balloons to $3,000 for the year, for example, than to ignore it for 10 years and let it climb to $30,000. Taking inventory is not necessarily fun, but it could save your money... hospital bills... and even your marriage.

10. *Get out of your own way:* It's hard to see ourselves as others see us, so we often misjudge our own strengths and weaknesses that are so obvious to our friends, family, and co-workers. Like it or not, we all have our blind spots, that is, certain personality traits or dispositions that undermine our effectiveness at work... at home... and even at play. To Be the Boss of Me, you have to "get out of your own way" by recognizing your deficiencies and incorporating strategies to compensate for your blind spots. For example, I used to think I was flexible and easy going and respectful of other people's time. Then one day at work I flew into the office of my assistant and one of my partners with MY list of things that needed to be done to complete MY project. I got an earful, and it changed my perception of myself: In very direct, but necessary, language, they both let me know they were fed up with my interruptions and MY demands that they drop everything and attend to MY needs and MY compulsion to micro-manage every detail of MY projects. I was shocked. I had no idea how compulsive I was and how it negatively impacted others. I either had to get out of my own way, or they were going to push me out of the way. That day was an eye-opener for me, and I've gotten better about respecting others' time and parameters.

Your Bucket List

The hit movie *The Bucket List* was about two old guys with terminal cancer who made a list of exciting things they were going to do before they "kicked the bucket." I would hope that Be the Boss of Me was at the top of your bucket list.

To start your journey on your way to building resilience through self-reliance, I'll leave you with a four-panel cartoon from *Mother Goose and Grimm* by Mike Peters, syndicated in my local paper:

Panel 1: The not-too-smart Boston terrier, Ralph, is holding a pen and staring at a blank sheet of paper. He says, "I'm going to make a 'Bucket List' of all the wonderful things I've always wanted to do."

Panel 2: He writes "1." at the top of the page.

Panel 3: Looking puzzled, he stares at the number 1, which is blank.

Panel 4: He writes frantically, "1. Buy a bucket."

Go buy a bucket. Then get busy becoming the Boss of You.

The Safest Ships
Are Relationships

The Safest Ships
Are Relationships

Call it a club, call it a network, call it a tribe,
call it a family. Whatever you call it, whoever
you are, you need one.
—**Jane Howard**
writer

The healthiest city in the U.S. in the 1950s and '60s was Roseta, Pennsylvania, a village of 1,500 settled and populated by Italian immigrants in the late 1800s. The men worked mostly in a nearby slate mine, and the women worked making blouses, and over time, stores and bakeries popped up along Main Street.

What set Roseta apart from the thousands of similarly populated towns sprinkled across the country was one startling statistic: *Virtually no one from Roseta under the age of 55 showed signs of heart disease or died of a heart attack.* Furthermore, there was no suicide... no alcoholism... no drug addiction... no ulcers... no one on welfare, and little crime.

"These people were dying of old age. That's all," observed Dr. Stewart Wolf, who studied the "Roseta Effect" for a decade. In the 1950s, heart attacks were the leading cause of death in men under 65. Yet the citizens of Roseta seemed to be immune. Why? Dr. Wolf's research eventually uncovered the health secrets of the residents of Roseta.

Wolf originally theorized that the longevity resulted from one or more of three things: a healthier diet, an active lifestyle, or great genes. He was wrong. None of these variables applied to Roseta. In fact, Rosetans were living *exceptionally* unhealthy lifestyles: The women cooked with lard instead of the healthier olive oil, and the typical meal was loaded with cholesterol-packed sausages, pepperoni, salami, ham, and eggs; the men heavily smoked unfiltered cigarettes and walked only when necessary. Not surprisingly, obesity was common for both sexes.

As for good genes, Dr. Wolf discovered that relatives living back in Italy or in different parts of the U.S. were no healthier than the average American. Dr. Wolf finally concluded that the secret of Roseta had nothing to do with physical advantages, such as their diet or exercise or genes or the town's location. It had to do with the *emotional advantage* of a "powerful, protective social structure that insulated the citizens from the pressures of the outside world," writes Malcolm Gladwell in his bestseller, *Outliers*.

Relationships to the Rescue

After much research, Dr. Wolf learned that what set Roseta apart from the typical U.S. town was the town itself—the *community* that the sons and daughters of Italian immigrants set up to support each other. For example, Roseta had 22 different civic organizations in a town of under 2,000 people, so there were always meaningful meetings and events to attend with family and long-time friends. Extended families were the rule in Roseta, with, typically, three generations living in the same house. The residents sat on front porches and chatted with passersby on their way to shop at the many bakeries and meat shops in the heart of town, where they often lingered, talking and laughing, until the dinner hour chased them home. They attended mass at Our Lady of Mount Carmel and met afterwards to cook for one another. The wealthier residents didn't flaunt their wealth and helped the less fortunate without fanfare.

In a word, the residents of Roseta *cared* for their family and friends and neighbors. And the caring—and being cared about—made them healthy.

That's why I say that *the safest ships are relationships*—healthy, real relationships are good for both the "care-er" and the "care-ee" because both parties feel connected to an "ecosystem" larger and richer than their individual lives. "No man is an island," wrote John Donne nearly 400 years ago. His words foreshadow a description of the Roseta Effect:

No man is an island,

Entire of itself.

Each is a piece of the continent,

A part of the main.

Each man's death diminishes me,

For I am involved in mankind.

Therefore, send not to know

For whom the bell tolls,

It tolls for thee.

The residents of Roseta lived by Donne's axiom that no man is an island, and, as a result, their hearts and their health bounced while the health of people in similar towns and in similar situations broke. As we have learned from the people of Roseta, there are three key relationships that, if they are properly honored and nurtured, can increase your resilience:

1) Relationship with your *spouse*

2) Relationships with your *family and friends*

3) Relationships with *co-workers*

Let's take a moment to look at how resilient people honor and nurture each of these.

How to Improve Our Spousal Relationships

Back when I was teaching high school in the '70s and '80s, I'd occasionally have the good fortune to share my lunch hour with a grandmotherly substitute teacher named Opal. Opal admitted to being in her mid-70s, but she had the energy and passion of a young teacher. One of the few times I saw sadness cross her face was when she talked about having been happily married for 45 years and widowed for the last dozen. It was during that conversation that Opal said something I've never forgotten, even though the conversation occurred more than 25 years ago.

"A good marriage is the closest thing there is to heaven on earth," she said flatly, a statement so obvious to her that it didn't require emphasis.

I agree.

And I'm sure in their heart of hearts, everyone would love to have a slice of heaven on earth, yet half the marriages in the U.S. end up in divorce. Why is it that so many marriages start out so right and end up so wrong?

Well, we've all heard the usual advice: Don't try to change your partner… compromise… communicate… help around the house… set aside time for yourselves… choose your battles… never go to bed mad. Good advice, all of this. But in my view, the best advice comes from my friend Opal, who said this when I asked her the secret to a great marriage:

"It's important to choose the right partner, but it's more important to *be* the right partner. Too many people focus on changing the wrong person," she said. *Choosing* the right partner and, more importantly, *being* the right partner—I'd say that's the one-two punch for a knockout marriage.

The Little Things Are the Big Things

From reflecting on my own marriage and talking to my long-married friends, I think the biggest threat to long-term marriages results from our partner's little, regular annoying habits, like leaving dirty socks on the floor and the toilet seat up. These unnerving habits may seem small to the perpetrators, especially to most men, but to women, ignoring their repeated requests translates to "you do not listen to me… you do not respect me… you do not care about me." Marriage counselors and researchers who study marriages say that most marriages survive the occasional big setbacks, such as a job loss or illness, because people come together and support each other in times of crisis.

It's those annoying, everyday, "I-get-so-tired-of-telling-you" habits that, over time, erode the underpinnings of marriage like a steady drip of water on sandstone. Until one day, somebody wants out.

Here's a lesson I've learned the hard way. If something is a big thing to your spouse, no matter how trivial you think it might be, then treat it like a BIG thing. If it's a big thing to them, then in their minds, it is a big thing, no matter how you feel about it. Oh, and do whatever needs to be done without smirking. Or rolling your eyes. Or reminding your spouse in a sarcastic voice just how dutiful you are. Just do your duty, like an adult. That's what my friend Opal meant when she advised spouses to "*be* the right partner."

Essence of Great Relationships with Family and Friends

I've done a lot of thinking about the essence of good relationships… about what resides at the center of our love and respect for friends and family members. And the best way to explain that essence is to tell you a true story about two friends of mine, Jeff and Bill, who were best buddies even though they were very different in a very important phase of their lives.

Jeff was a dyed-in-the-wool conservative republican. He despised the Clintons... decried big government... and defended free-market capitalism as the end-all and be-all of democracy.

Bill, on the other hand, was a liberal democrat who often ran for local elected offices. He defended Clinton as a good president with some bad habits that, in Bill's view, had nothing to do with Clinton's ability to govern... championed massive government programs for the disadvantaged... and defended higher taxes for the lucky few who benefited most from capitalism.

As I said, they were polar opposites when it came to politics. But guess who headed up Bill's fundraising when he ran for office as a democrat? You guessed it—his republican friend Jeff.

Several years ago, Bill was diagnosed with incurable cancer. The person who grieved the most other than Bill's family was his friend Jeff, who was devastated. Several years after Bill's passing, I was having lunch with Jeff when I asked him, "Jeff, how could you and Bill remain best friends even though you were on totally opposite sides politically?"

Jeff gave me a withering, disbelieving look, as if I'd just reached over and taken a bite of his sandwich without asking.

"Steve, it's only politics," he scoffed.

Then he turned his attention back to his lunch, as if my question was so beyond the pale it didn't deserve acknowledgment, much less further discussion.

Jeff's comment summed up my feelings that the essence of friendship is *acceptance*—acceptance for your friends and family to be themselves, even if their "self" runs contrary to your values and world view. I have many friends who are not only different, they're certifiably odd to the point of being eccentric. That's okay by me. In their view, I'm the oddball. But because my friends and I accept each other to the point of celebrating our differences, our friendships have lasted decades. (On the opposite side of the acceptance ledger, a woman I've known for more than 20 years—an acquaintance of mine, but most certainly not a friend—has cut ties with four of her closest friends because they dared to disagree with her. Hope she runs out of disagreements before she runs out of friends.)

One of the things I'm proudest of in my life is the fact that over the years, my friends and I have had career changes... geographical changes... political changes... even religious changes, but our friendships have remained unchanged.

Relationships with Co-Workers

At the end of the day, every business is a people business. If you can't get along with people... if you can't manage and motivate people at work and at home, you've signed up for some misery in this life. It's impossible to bounce if all your relationships are broken.

But you don't need an MBA in management to get people to like you and to do what you want them to do. In fact, recent research has shown that there's a segment of the population with only 8th-grade educations that are more successful in business than most college graduates.

We're talking about the Amish.

Yep, you read it right, the Amish, those quaint, horse-and-buggy, straw-hat-and-suspenders people looking like they walked off a Currier and Ives dinner plate. What could they possibly teach us about modern management?

Plenty.

According to a new study in the *Global Business and Economics Review*, only 10% of Amish businesses fail in their first five years, well below the failure rate of non-Amish small businesses in the U.S. How can people who reject cars, electricity, and telephones in their homes do so well in the modern marketplace when competitors are armed with smart phones and laptops?

The answer can be found in a recent book, *Success Made Simple: An Inside Look at Why Amish Businesses Thrive*, by Erik Wesner, a former sales manager who lived and worked among the Amish for five years. Wesner says the key to the enviable success record of Amish businessmen is attributable in the main to their simple, sincere response to relationships.

"One thing I heard consistently was the comment from Amish owners, 'I'd never ask an employee to do something that I wouldn't be willing to do myself,' said Wesner. "It's like a mantra to them. They will exhibit that by jumping in sometimes and doing the dirty work. Employees notice, and it makes an impact."

One Amish builder occasionally takes all 18 of his employees to breakfast. He not only picks up the tab, but he also pays his employees for the time spent at the restaurant. As a result, his employees have stayed with him an average of nine years each. The loyalty spills over to his customers, too, because the Amish value long-term relationships over one-time deals.

The Family That Works Together, Stays Together

The Amish men also show their commitment to relationships by seeking out work that enables them to spend time with their wives and children. One man Wesner interviewed admitted his work making wire hairpins at home was tedious, but he had turned down higher-paying and more fulfilling work to be around the people who mean the most to him.

"I enjoy being with my wife and kids so we can work together," said 36-year-old Daniel Fisher.

The Amish low-tech lifestyle is conducive to building and nurturing relationships, as evidenced by their zero divorce rate and rare separations among married couples. Contrast that to the typical U.S. household, where the average household consumes more than eight hours of TV per day, with 83% of homes owning multi-sets of two, three, four, or more TVs. No wonder the divorce rate is 50%.

People seeking a healthy life… and a healthy family… and a healthy business would be wise to go "back to the future" by returning to the lifestyle in the village of Roseta in the 1950s and the values of the Amish today. They understand that it's a lot easier to bounce when you know someone you love is there to catch you when you fall.

RESILIENT RULE 7:

To Grow More, You Must Know More

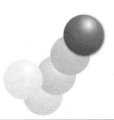

To Grow More, You Must Know More

An investment in knowledge pays the best interest.
—Benjamin Franklin

I never let my schooling interfere with my education.
—Mark Twain

S*top the World—I Want to Get Off* was the title of a popular Broadway play in the early 1960s. It's also an apt description of how we feel in this hurly-burly, fast-changing world. We just want things we can't control to STOP!

Stop stock market plunges.

Stop foreclosures.

Stop layoffs.

Stop terrorism.

Stop government spending.

Stop inflation.

Stop political infighting.

Stop illegal immigration.

Stop outsourcing.

Stop banks too big to fail.

Stop oil spills that pollute our environment.

I expect you have a few other items you'd like to add to this "stopping list." News flash!—as much as we'd sometimes like to be Jim Carrey's omnipotent character in the movie *Bruce Almighty*, we can't bend the world to our will. As Czech author Franz Kafka observed decades ago, "In a battle between you and the world, bet on the world."

Knowledge Helps Us Maneuver in the World

No, we can't control the world. But we *can* control our **knowledge** of the world. Knowledge is our biggest lever to move our advantage in the world, but we aren't born with knowledge. We have to seek it. No one was born knowing how to balance a checkbook or fix a leaky faucet or design an iPhone. All those tasks require knowledge that enables people to solve problems and do their jobs and get along—and get ahead—in the world. The overriding question for people today is, "In a global economy that is getting more connected and changing faster with each passing day, how do we stay ahead of the curve?"

The one-word answer: Knowledge. The more we know, the more we can grow in all phases of our lives—in business… in our personal relationships… in our maturity… the list is endless.

Tom Peters, best-selling author and respected consultant to businesses around the globe, tells the story of having Sunday dinner at his girlfriend's house when he was a senior in high school. After dinner, the girl's father, a very successful doctor, excused himself and retired to his home office, where he spent the next three hours preparing for the week ahead. The soon-to-graduate Peters realized at that moment that "homework never ends if you want to be a success in life."

We all want success in life—that's obvious—but we can't be successful unless we have the **knowledge and know-how** that customers, clients, partners, or employers are willing to pay us for. So, let's take a brief look at the basic ways of acquiring the knowledge that will give us a leg up in the world.

Read and Get Rich

Back in 1998, I did the research for a mega-selling book, *Read and Get Rich*. In the chapter titled, *The Readers and the Read-Nots vs. The Haves and the Have-Nots*, we pointed out that 20% of Americans are functionally illiterate, which, in the Information Age, virtually dooms them to a life of menial labor, at best. But even more distressing are the 30% who can read reasonably well but choose NOT to read. As Mark Twain observed, "The man who does not read good books has no advantage over the man who cannot read them."

The math is appalling: Add the 20% illiterates to the 30% Read-Nots, and we end up with half the adult population who fail to read a single book during any given year. Just think—half the population has been handed the greatest tool for self-improvement ever invented, and they refuse to use it. It's like being handed the combination to a safe deposit box containing a million dollars and the secret to happiness, and just tossing it into the trash.

Most people's biggest excuse for not reading is lack of time. Oh, really? Yet the average person has the time to watch eight hours of television a day, seven days a week, on three or more sets sprinkled around the house. Truth is, people don't have to choose between watching TV and reading books—they can do both. The typical one-hour TV show has 16 minutes of commercials, which means viewers could read a dozen books a year if they'd read during the commercial breaks of their nightly hour of "must-see TV."

Don't believe it? Here's the math:

The average high school graduate reads 250 words per minute, so, to allow for distractions, let's reduce the average to 200 words per minute. There are 400 or so words on this page, which means if you're an average reader, it would take you two minutes to read this page. At that rate you can read about seven pages in a 15-minute span. But let's reduce it to the ridiculous and say the typical person will read only five pages in 15 minutes.

This book has a little more than 100 numbered pages, including the introduction and conclusion. By reading just five pages a day, you could easily finish this book in 20 days. By the end of the year, you could read a dozen books this size and squeeze in a few short mysteries, to boot. And that's reading slowly for only 15 minutes a day.

Don't have time to read? Try a different excuse.

Driving Home the Value of Reading

In case you're still skeptical that you can "read and get rich" investing only 15 minutes a day, I'd like to tell you about Tim Driggers, a school bus driver in Tampa who is enriching his passengers' lives—and his own—by reading to, and with, the elementary school students on his bus while they wait 15 to 20 minutes before the school doors open each day.

Driggers and about 20 regular bus riders have read dozens of books in the past two years. They take turns reading as Driggers quizzes them to make sure they're paying attention, and he engages them by asking for predictions about what's about to happen in the story. The whole bus applauds each time a student is done reading.

Driggers is an unlikely reading teacher. He failed fourth grade, and, by his own admission, was never much of a reader. Then one day he found a book on an empty seat of his bus. No one claimed it, so he started reading it to the kids in the morning. After the first day, they were hooked: Non-readers have started reading on their own. Slow readers have picked up speed. And quiet kids are joining in conversations.

Even Driggers has picked up the reading habit, reading for a couple of hours in the afternoon before dropping the kids off after school. In May of 2010, the International Reading Association presented Celebrate Literacy Awards for Hillsborough County, where Tampa is located. Among the recipients were principals, reading specialists, reading coaches—and one bus driver named Tim Driggers.

He got the only standing ovation of the evening.

Driggers understands that reading can make you rich in more ways than money. He and his students are growing rich together. With each new book they read, he sees growth in the students and growth in himself as a leader... as a teacher... and as a person.

Now, that's worth a standing ovation.

What Are You Watering in Your Garden?

Excuses are easy to find and they breed like rabbits: *I'm too old... I'm too young... I'm too tired... I'm too wired... I'm too broke... I'm too rich... yada, yada, yada.* Excuses are like weeds—if you water them, they will starve out the growth of the healthy things in your life.

I'm going to tell you four brief stories about people who had some great excuses NOT to learn... to just throw up their hands and stay mired down in the quicksand of underachievement. But because they didn't let excuses hold them back from getting the knowledge that opened doors for them, they have grown personally and professionally.

Alice Thomas, a prosperous real estate executive, got disgusted with TV's portrayal of older adults as "doddering fools," so she decided to put herself through law school to work on behalf of elderly clients. In May of 2010, Thomas, accepted her law degree from the Pacific McGeorge School of Law. She was 79.

Jay Trezevant, an assistant U.S. attorney in Tampa, is regarded as one of the toughest, best-prepared prosecutors in the country, despite being a quadriplegic, the result of a high school diving accident: "The best way to overcome disabilities is through education," says Trezevant. "Through education you can become independent, and you can maximize any potential you have. With education, you can go places you can't even imagine."

Stephen J. Cannell, TV producer, writer, and novelist, has struggled with dyslexia so severe that he barely graduated from high school and must dictate scripts and books to an assistant because his spelling is so atrocious. Yet he learned his craft as a writer for TV shows and went on to earn millions writing pilots for TV that went on to become hits, including *The Rockford Files*, *The A-Team*, and *Hunter*.

Gabrielle Lozano, 20, graduated from a culinary arts program in the summer of 2010 with the dream of opening her own sandwich and bake shop, a lofty goal for any 20-year-old but especially ambitious for Gabrielle, who is blind.

"She is beyond awesome," says school director Mary Cantrell. "She works with her other senses and never once considers herself handicapped."

By acquiring knowledge that has value in the marketplace, these people were able to grow and prosper despite having to overcome physical challenges. Their achievements remind us that if they're resilient enough to achieve their goals, we can certainly achieve ours.

Even at the Top, You Can Always Learn More

Here's yet another amazing story about how someone grew professionally by acquiring the necessary knowledge to change careers, even though he was earning millions of dollars a year as a cardiologist.

In 2003, Dr. Delos Cosgrove was at the top of his game. He had spent 30 years as a heart surgeon, performing more than 22,000 operations at the prestigious Cleveland Clinic, the top cardiac hospital in the world. Although he was a millionaire many times over, at age 62, when most men are itching to retire, Dr. Cosgrove changed careers from surgeon to, of all things, CEO of the Cleveland Clinic.

"I went to business school when I realized I was going to have this opportunity," the now 69-year-old said. "I studied hard. I would work during the day, then go home and hit the books at night. I had a lot of people who were very generous with their advice—very successful, very high-level CEOs—and they were very generous with their time and their suggestions, and I'm grateful for that."

What's most amazing about Dr. Cosgrove's story was how humble he was for a man who was regarded as one of the leading surgeons at the top-rated hospital in the world. But he knew he needed more than just his skills as a surgeon to succeed as a CEO, so he sought out knowledge in books, from professors, and from seasoned mentors who could show him the ropes.

Get the Knowledge... Then Get Going Using It

"Knowledge is power," wrote Sir Francis Bacon nearly four centuries ago. He was close. Knowledge *put to use* is power. Otherwise, it's useless. Knowing is nice, but it's not enough. But when combined with action, knowledge can, to quote Jay Trezevant, "take us places you can't even imagine."

I understand the divide between getting knowledge and then putting it into action. For the past four years, I've been acquiring knowledge about investing in the stock market. I subscribe to six different investment newsletters and an equal number of business publications, including *Forbes*, *Fortune*, and *The Wall Street Journal*. Over that time I've certainly acquired enough knowledge to manage my own investment accounts.

Yet, I still pay a broker to oversee my investments, even though I make all the buying and selling decisions. Why? Insecurity, I suppose.

But my insecurity is costing me a lot of money that I could be reinvesting to make even more money for my family and me. It's foolish. It's indefensible. Yet, here I sit, too timid to take control, too *afraid*— yes, that's the only word to use, afraid—to trust my knowledge and take the action to manage my own financial affairs. So, I'm taking my own advice I gave in Chapter 5: *Be the Boss of 'Me.'* I'm announcing to my "friends" (in this case, the readers of this book) my intention to manage my investment accounts *by myself*, and I'm setting a deadline for myself to go solo.

Here's my commitment: On the date this book is published, I will call my investment advisor and switch my accounts from his brokerage to my online account at Scottrade.

There, I said it in print, and I'll do it in June.

The Fast and Easy Way to Estate Planning

I wish estate planning were as easy as a joke I recently read on the Internet. It goes like this: Dan was a shy, rather plain-looking single man working in the family business and living at home with his elderly father. When Dan discovered he was going to inherit millions when his sickly father died, he decided he needed a wife to share it with.

One evening at an investment meeting, Dan spotted the most beautiful woman he'd ever seen. He mustered up all his courage and approached her with this line:

"I may look like a simple, ordinary man to you," he stammered as he looked down at his shoes. "But in a very short time, my father will die, and I'll inherit 200 million dollars.

Impressed, the woman obtained Dan's business card, and three days later… she married his father.

Women are so much better at estate planning than men.

Persistence Beats Resistance

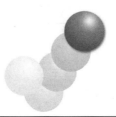

Persistence Beats Resistance

Pain is temporary. Quitting is forever.
—Lance Armstrong
7-time winner of the Tour de France

Peddling a bike for 100-plus miles in Florida's mid-summer heat and humidity is not most people's idea of a good time. "It's sometimes grueling," admits my friend Dick Woltman, who just turned 65. But he loves the physical challenge and trains for the occasional 100-miler by biking 20 miles at 6 a.m. on weekends and vacation days.

Dick is nothing if not determined and disciplined.

I remember talking with him after he completed a 125-mile ride during the peak of the Florida summer. Commenting on the ride, Dick made an observation that really stuck with me. He said he was approaching the 60-mile mark when he peddled past the tour's courtesy van loading up some young riders who were too exhausted to finish the ride.

"I felt sorry for those young guys," Dick said. "They looked to be 20-something and in good shape, but they quit before finishing the ride. What's sad is by quitting, these young guys will never know what it feels like to push past the pain and come out stronger on the other side."

Persisting through the Pain

Pushing past the pain—that's certainly one of the things resilient people do, whether it's physical pain... pain of rejection... pain of loss... or pain of heartbreak—resilient people push past the pain and come out on the other side.

I want to tell you a brief story about a young woman, Scout Bassett, who has pushed past ALL of these pains to become a college student and spokesperson for the Challenged Athletes Foundation.

When Scout, who was born in China, was less than a year old, she lost her right leg after suffering severe burns. Shortly afterward, she was abandoned at an orphanage, where, for the next seven years, she scrubbed floors, did laundry, and washed dishes. She was frequently beaten with a stick or a shoe whether she misbehaved or not. At age 7, she weighed 25 pounds, having eaten only rice and crackers since her birth. In 1997, she was adopted by a Michigan couple, but the transition from a cold, callous orphanage to a warm, loving home was anything but smooth.

She was overwhelmed by culture shock. She couldn't speak English... had never heard music... never seen a book or a magazine... never ridden in a car... never stayed in a hotel... never eaten in a restaurant. What seems ordinary to us was terrifying to young Scout. She cried. She fought. She screamed. The first years were tough on everyone.

But Scout learned to adjust. By fifth grade, she finished second in a statewide spelling bee. And she discovered sports. Although she grew to only 4-foot-8, with the aid of a prosthetic leg she competed in tennis and golf in high school. She taught herself to swim so she could compete in triathlons.

China thinks of discarded or disabled children as "throwaways," destined to be beggars. But in the states, we think of Scout Bassett as a "keeper." By the way, the original orphanage in China has been torn down. But Scout is still standing tall, thanks to her perseverance through the pain.

Rejecting Rejection

In the world of business, most notably publishing, one person's *rejection* is another person's *rejoicing*. Some of the most profitable books of all time were rejected by publisher after publisher before a perceptive reader in the publishing chain spotted a talent the others missed.

Here are a few blockbuster books that were rejected by most publishing "professionals" which became bestsellers because someone believed in the books enough to persevere until they were published:

- Anne Frank's *Diary of a Young Girl* had been published in Holland shortly after WWII and sold moderately well. The English-translated manuscript was rejected by 15 publishers before an alert assistant in the Paris office of Doubleday Publishing disobeyed her boss' orders to reject the book and sent it to Doubleday's New York editors. Published in the States in 1952, to date the book has sold 30 million copies in dozens of languages.

- The first title of Joseph Heller's *Catch-22* was *Catch-18*, but Heller changed the title because his manuscript was rejected by 21 publishers before Simon and Schuster accepted it. *Catch-22* has become part of our everyday language and the book has sold 10 million copies over the years.

- *Chicken Soup for the Soul* was rejected by a record 140 publishers on the grounds it was "too positive" and "anthologies never sell" before a small, near-bankrupt publisher took a chance on the collection. Today, the 65-title series has sold more than 80 million copies in 40 languages.

- Sales of Dr. Seuss books have soared to more than 100 million now, but the first book of the series, *And to Think That I Saw It on Mulberry Street*, was rejected by 27 publishers before Vanguard Press saw something the others missed. Tens of millions of children around the world saw the same thing—silly stories with silly dialog and sillier illustrations make for great reading.

- The most profitable publishing success of all time, the *Harry Potter* series, was turned down by 12 publishers in the U.S. before Scholastic Books signed author J.K. Rowling to a multiple-book deal. The earnings from sales of the seven books (400 million copies in 67 countries), six movie versions, and tie-in merchandise are estimated to total a breathtaking $15 billion.

What would have happened if the authors and agents had given up after the first rejection... or second rejection... or third rejection... or fourth rejection, or, in the case of *Chicken Soup for the Soul*, the 140th rejection? The authors, publishers, and reading public would be a lot poorer, wouldn't they, proving that persistence produces profits.

Frustration Leads to Founding of Tea Party Movement

We learned in middle school that the first Tea Party originated in Boston in 1773, when enraged citizens protesting taxation without representation tossed tons of British tea into Boston Harbor.

The second Tea Party arrived 236 years later on the opposite coast, when Keli Carender got tired of politicians throwing taxpayer money down the drain on ill-conceived "stimulus programs." In the fall of 2009, when Carender tried calling her senators to urge them to vote against the $787 billion stimulus bill, she found their voice mailboxes were full. She decided to hold her own protest against what she called "porkulus."

"I thought to myself, I have two courses I can take," she said to an interviewer. "I can give up, go home, crawl into bed, be really depressed, and let this thing happen. Or, I can do something different, and I can find a new avenue to have my voice be heard."

She chose to be heard by organizing a protest.

Her first rally drew 120 people in Seattle. A week later, it grew to 300. Six weeks later, 1,200 gathered for a Tax Day Tea Party. Only a year after her first rally, millions of Americans assembled in cities across the country to protest lavish government spending on programs that do little more than dig the country deeper into debt. The movement portends a huge defeat for tax-and-spend Washington politicians in the coming election.

The tone-deaf politicians may have been more powerful, but Carender was more persistent, and in the end, *persistence beats resistance*—even on Capitol Hill.

A Marine and His Mutt

Persistence isn't just limited to humans, as evidenced by this next story about a Marine and a mixed-breed cur in Iraq named Nubs. In 2009, Major Brian Dennis was the leader of an 11-man U.S. Marine force patrolling the border between Iraq and Syria when the scruffy leader of a pack of wild dogs approached Dennis as he was eating MRE ("Meal-Ready-to-Eat")-prepared spaghetti. Dennis shared his meal, and the pair bonded immediately. Dennis named the dog "nubs" for his crudely hacked-off ears, and each time the Marines would revisit the area, Nubs would seek out his new buddy and hang out with the unit.

When Dennis took his patrol 75 miles north of their usual encampment, Nubs chased after his truck until he collapsed exhausted in the road. Dennis thought he'd seen his canine friend for the last time. But two days later, a Marine came to Dennis and announced, "You'll never guess who's outside."

It was Nubs, limping, bitten, and scarred from fights with wolves and rival dog packs. He had traveled over a rock-strewn desert—broiling hot in the day, sub-freezing at night—to track down his new friend. Although it's against military policy for active personnel to befriend found animals, Dennis found a loophole—there was no policy against *shipping* animals.

Dennis recalls, "I looked at him and thought, 'This little guy has earned a trip to America.'"

Dennis appealed for donations from friends and family back home, raising $5,000 to fund the trip. It took a month to get Nubs from Iraq to San Diego, where Dennis lives. First stop was Amman, Jordan, then a 10-hour flight to Chicago, where he stayed with friends of one of Dennis' sympathetic officers. Then on to San Diego, where Nubs stayed with more friends until Dennis' tour of duty was over.

The resilience and resolve displayed by both a man and a dog struck a chord with pet-crazy Americans, and Nubs and his owner have made appearances on *Today* and *The Tonight Show*. Dennis turned his story into a children's book, *Nubs: The Story of a Mutt, a Marine, and a Miracle*, and Warner Brothers is beginning production on the movie version.

A Fight to the End

One of my favorite novels is *The Old Man and the Sea* by Ernest Hemingway. It's the story of an impoverished old fisherman in Cuba who hooks a giant marlin, and after an exhausting two-day battle, lands the record fish by himself. The marlin is too big to fit in the boat, so he lashes it to the side, but on the way back to land, sharks devour the fish. In Hemingway's eyes, the old man is a hero even though his trophy fish is lost because of the *courageous and correct way* he fought the battle.

The next story I'd like to tell you reminds me of *The Old Man and the Sea* because of the way the hero—in this case, the heroine—fought her battle in life correctly, with courage and perseverance. Diagnosed with cystic fibrosis at 6 weeks old, Mallory Code refused to fall victim to the disease, even though her life expectancy was 16 to 18 years.

Code eventually succumbed to the disease at age 25, but she packed a lifetime into her shortened life, accomplishing more in her 25 years than most people lucky enough to live three times longer. She played the piano, performed in ballet and tap dancing recitals, and took up golf, where she excelled, winning numerous junior tournaments and earning a scholarship to the University of Florida, from which she graduated.

Cystic fibrosis is a chronic lung disease that makes victims vulnerable to infections, especially pneumonia and blood infections. A month before her death, Code checked herself out of an Orlando hospital and drove back to Tampa so she could attend the long-planned birthday party of her beloved 1-year-old niece. She passed away in a Tampa hospital, fighting to the end.

Not surprisingly, Code became a much-sought-after motivational speaker, and her stirring message emphasized remaining positive and persistent, even in face of the inevitable:

"Some days I feel like I've climbed a mountain, and I get to the top, and I see a whole mountain range before me that I still have to climb," she said to a rapt audience. "I handle it with a little bit of humor, and a little bit of tears and some of both. My life is perfect in almost every way. I've got this awesome family, awesome friends, and an awesome relationship with the Lord Jesus. I've got golf, dance, everything. I don't want to be thought of as the little sick girl out there."

You Cannot Defeat Me

At a time when many people just sleepwalk through life, accepting government handouts, getting by on minimum effort accompanied by maximum complaining, Mallory Code reminds us how precious and brief life is and she inspires us to achieve more and *be* more. Her determination and spirit remind me of the opening stanza to a famous Dylan Thomas poem the author wrote encouraging his aging father never to resign in life but to fight to the bitter end.

> Do not go gentle into that good night,
> Old age should burn and rage at close of day;
> Rage, rage against the dying of the light.

Mallory Code did not accept her fate gently. She danced and golfed and bounced from hospital room to hospital room, determined to rage against the dying of the light until her last breath. She personifies the advice that Ann Landers said was the most important advice she ever gave in a career that spanned nearly half a century:

"If I were asked to give what I consider the single most useful bit of advice for all of humanity, it would be this: Expect trouble as an inevitable part of life, and when it comes, hold your head high, look it squarely in the eye, and say, *'I will be bigger than you. You cannot defeat me.'*"

Death took Mallory Code, but it did not defeat her.

When my time comes, I pray that I'm as persistent, and as brave, as she.

RESILIENT RULE 9:

Character Counts

Character Counts

Character is doing what's right when nobody is looking.
There are too many people who think the only thing that's
right is to get by, and the only thing wrong is to get caught.
—J.C. Watts
former GOP congressman

T iger Woods, Bill Clinton, and Bernie Madoff discovered the hard way this timeless truth—*character counts.*

All three men were at the top of their games… rich, powerful, revered by millions. Then the truth came out, as it always does. And they discovered they couldn't talk themselves out of something they'd behaved themselves into.

"Character is higher than intellect," said Emerson. "A great soul will be strong in living as well as strong in thinking." Clinton and Madoff (and millions more like them) have exceptional intellect, as does Tiger Woods, whose otherworldly focus and mental toughness certainly must qualify as superior intellect on the field of athletics.

Yet their lack of character led to scandals and public disgrace, proving that Emerson is right: Character counts precisely because character is higher than intellect.

Why Character Is Under Siege

Webster's New World Dictionary defines character as *"moral constitution; moral strength; self-discipline, fortitude, etc."* In a nutshell, character is knowing the difference between right and wrong and then always trying to do what's right.

But today, character is under attack by the Culture of Now, a time in history when, for more and more people, "doing the right thing" has become a nuisance that just gets in the way of instant gratification. It's as if much of the world suddenly inherited Attention Deficit Disorder, caving in to the childish urge to get what we want *(everything!)* when we want it *(right now!)*. In the Culture of Now, the long-term ethos of established religions—"getting right with your maker"—has been replaced with the short-term mantra of secularism—"getting rich..." "getting famous"... "getting ahead"... "getting mine"... and "getting away with it." In the Culture of Now, the end justifies the means: rich is rich, whether the money is made from owning grocery stores or operating gambling casinos.

Forgotten Missions

Peggy Noonan, columnist for *The Wall Street Journal*, says the Culture of Now has caused major institutions to forget their mission: "Institutions that everyday help hold us together acted as if they had forgotten their mission, forgotten what they were about, what their role and purpose was, what they existed to do in the first place."

Examples are abundant: *Wall Street's mission* of providing an economic footing for the U.S. and much of the world was replaced by the rush to "earn" giant bonuses by selling junk securities to unsuspecting investors. *Congress' mission* of legislating with a long view for the citizenry was replaced by their spend-now, worry-about-it-later mentality. *The public school's mission* to teach and guide our youth was replaced by union demands for secure jobs and higher pay based 100% on seniority and 0% on competence.

Noonan aptly sums up the outcome: "And as all these institutions forgot their mission, they entered the empire of spin. They turned more and more attention, resources, and efforts to the public perception of their institution and not to the reality of it."

Okay, a lot of people took wrong turns in the first decade of the new millennium.

That's the bad news.

The good news—character is making a comeback, as evidenced by the launch of a new non-profit concept from Panera Bread, a national bakery and restaurant chain.

What Would You Pay?

Panera Bread has expanded to 1,400 locations across the country by offering a healthy alternative to fast food—hearty soups and heart-healthy sandwiches instead of coronary-clogging burgers and fries. The food is healthier and the atmosphere is trendier at Panera, which is why customers are willing to pay a bit more than they'd pay at Burger King or McDonald's. But in a daring experiment, Panera launched a new non-profit store in an upscale suburb of St. Louis that offers the same menu as the other locations, but the prices are different—a lot different.

There aren't any.

Customers are told to donate what they want for a meal, whether that's the full-suggested "donation," or a penny, or a $100. The pilot restaurant, named the St. Louis Bread Company after its hometown location, is run by a non-profit foundation. The foundation pays the new restaurant's bills, including staff salaries, rent, and food costs. At the end of each month, donations will be tallied against costs. Any profits will be used to keep the restaurant running and to support future locations and training programs for at-risk youth.

Other similar restaurant models offering pay-what-you-want menus have worked. One World in Salt Lake City has operated as a non-profit since 2003. "It somehow stays in balance," says Denise Cerreta, founder of One World." I think, ultimately, people are good. They want to contribute."

These restaurants are proof that the vast majority of people believe character counts, and they act accordingly. If unscrupulous people outnumbered people with character, these restaurants would fold after a month. But for every person who underpays for a meal, there are two or three or more who compensate by overpaying because they love the honesty and openness engendered in the pay-what-you-can concept.

Doing Good Is Good for Business

Obviously, not every business lends itself to the pay-what-you-can concept. Can you imagine what would happen if a car dealer made the same offer? People without principles would be lined up around the block, snatching up SUVs for a buck or two.

But recent research shows that character counts for businesses, as well as individuals, in everyday life. According to *Fortune* magazine, "… companies that 'outbehave' their competitors ethically will also tend to outperform them financially." This is especially true today, as globalization has made it increasingly difficult for companies to compete solely on the lowest price. No matter what the product, someone, somewhere, will likely be able to copy it and sell it for less.

"All the more important, then, for companies to compete at the level of behavior, especially how they treat employees and customers," says *Fortune*. Which means trust, kindness, empathy, and overall goodness—in a word, good character—will be the "soft currency" of the 21st century.

The rise of instant information via the Internet and 24/7 vigilance via cell phone cameras and ubiquitous video monitoring makes good behavior more important because it has become harder to hide bad behavior. Prior to the 1990s, Hollywood, the rich and famous, or large companies used public relations departments to counter and control bad news.

But today, in the age of instant information, it becomes hard to control a story, so the methods for controlling the message in the past—denying, lying, and stonewalling (which may have worked for Tiger Woods to control his scandal in past decades)—backfires today. The more that guilty parties deny, the more the media digs, making a deeper and deeper hole to bury the brand in.

The message for businesses is "Today people can see into your life farther, faster, and cheaper than ever before," says Dov Seidman, author of How: *Why How We Do Anything Means Everything in Business (and in Life).* In effect, we're all on *Candid Camera,* and the world is watching. So be on your best behavior at all times.

The Reality of Redemption

But what happens when people or organizations do mess up? Let's face it, sometime, somewhere, all individuals—you and me included—and all organizations are going to make mistakes. Then what?

"There are no second acts in America," observed the great American novelist F. Scott Fitzgerald, meaning that anyone who messes up was instantly a social outcast doomed for the dumpster.

He was wrong.

The only thing Americans (and much of the rest of the world) enjoy more than watching the rich and famous fall off Mt. Olympus is watching them redeem themselves and retain, or surpass, their former achievements. But for redemption to occur, the fallen must publicly recognize and renounce their past transgressions and *undergo a change of character.*

The formula for redemption goes like this: When you goof up, then just admit it… take responsibility… apologize… ask for forgiveness… be sincere about changing your behavior… and then, most importantly, *change your behavior,* and get on with your life. (Are you listening, Tiger?—be sincere and *change your behavior!*)

Two classic examples of redemption are Paul's conversion from a persecutor of Christians to a preacher of the gospel and Captain John Newton's conversion from a captain of a slave ship to a humble priest and composer of the much-beloved hymn, *Amazing Grace*; Newton's despicable past adds meaning to his stirring first verse, "Amazing grace, how sweet the sound, that saved a wretch like me. I once was lost, but now I'm found, was blind but now I see."

Two recent examples of redeemed reputations are Robert Downey, Jr., star of *Ironman* and *Sherlock Holmes*; and Glenn Beck, talk radio and cable TV host. Let's look at Downey first.

Downey is a super-talented Academy Award-nominated actor who fell into alcohol and drug abuse in the 1990s. He was in and out of jail and rehab so often that directors couldn't trust him to be sober or available for scenes, so he went without work for several years. Eventually, he sobered up and wised up, changed his habits, changed his circle of friends, and started working again. For the last three years he's been the top box-office draw in Hollywood, earning his pictures, and himself, millions.

Downey's redemption is traceable to one key word—*trust*. He's always oozed with talent. When he was serving time in jail... or sequestered in a rehab clinic, he still had his talent, but what he didn't have was trustworthiness. Without that, talent means nothing because directors and producers couldn't *trust* Downey would be available to use that talent. For the last 10 years, Downey appears to have made a turnaround. No drunken driving charges. No drug busts. No cancelled appearances. Just a lot of good work in a lot of good movies. For his sake, I hope his redemption is permanent.

Glenn Beck, 46, is the poster boy for the Tea Party movement, but no one who knew him in his 30s would have guessed this reformed alcoholic would be hosting a top-rated TV show on FOX, writing best-selling books, and touring the country to sold-out audiences while earning upwards of $40 million a year. In any given month, he reaches 30 million listeners and viewers.

"By the time I was 30," he says, "nobody would work with me. I was friendless, I was hopeless, I was suicidal, lost my family—I mean it was bad." Beck credits Alcoholics Anonymous, a supportive wife, and religion with turning his life around. The key to his redemption and newfound success stems from the same character trait that redeemed Robert Downey, Jr.—trust. You may like or dislike Beck. You may agree or disagree with him. But you can *trust him to be himself* and to deliver his message with passion and purpose every single broadcast, every single day. His commercial time is for sale, but his message isn't.

That's character.

A Call for a Culture of Character

For more than a decade, conservative talk-radio host Dennis Prager has been broadcasting that character counts at all levels in society, from the individual... to the family... to government... to corporations... to our laws... to our educational system... to our justice system... to the way we dress... to the music we listen to. Here is Prager's challenge that we return to a Culture of Character:

> The most important question a society can ask is how to raise young people to be good adults. Before we can train people to become social activists or Wall Street bankers, first they must learn basic character traits—truth telling, financial honesty, humility, honoring their parents, and above all else, self control. There is no federal budget, no senate or house bill, no social policy, no healthcare fix that can do as much good as a society that is filled with decent people.

Who wouldn't want to be surrounded by decent people? I would—and, for the most part, I am. I'd like to think I'm a person of character (although that wasn't the case when I was younger), and if the quality of friends and your spouse are any indication of character, then I'm doing something right. I think it's a bonus that character can increase profits for companies and individuals, but as I see it, that's an ancillary advantage of good character, not the reason we should seek to be a person of high character.

In the final analysis, character is its own reward. And that reward will lead to a life well-lived, best described by Bessie A. Stanley in an oft-reprinted short essay titled, *What Is Success?*, first published in 1911.

What Is Success?

To laugh often and much; to win the respect of intelligent people and affection of children; to earn the appreciation of honest critics and endure the betrayal of false friends; to appreciate beauty, to find the best in others; to leave the world a bit better, whether by a healthy child, a garden patch, or redeemed social condition; to know even one life has breathed easier because you have lived. This is to have succeeded.

A message as timeless as character itself.

Take Your Own Advice

Take Your Own Advice

We are all wise for other people, seldom for ourselves.
—Ralph Waldo Emerson

"**D**o *you know what a personal crisis is? It's the opportunity to take your own advice.*"

I can't remember when, or where, I first read or heard that comment... I can't remember whether it was delivered as a joke or sarcastic remark... I can't remember whether it was said by a character in a movie or a book or a grandstanding politician during a TV interview.

Nope—I don't remember any of the particulars.

But I do remember being knocked back in my chair by the universal truth of that statement—or perhaps I should say, by the *personal truth of that statement*—as it winged straight from the source to my solar plexus—bam! The unerring accuracy of that statement—*a personal crisis is an opportunity to take your own advice*—was aimed at me.

And it nailed me, Mr. Opinionated, right in the gut.

Too Free with My Advice

I've always been free with my advice to others, oftentimes to the annoyance of my friends, and, not infrequently, total strangers. Maybe it stems from my being a former teacher and coach, when classrooms and coaching required I give my younger, less experienced charges advice.

But I think it goes further back than that.

Some people are just free with their opinions on how others should conduct their lives. I'm one of those people. Not as bad as I used to be, for sure. Age and experience have softened me a bit. But if you drop a problem on my doorstep, without a moment's hesitation, I'll weigh in with a solution. That's just me being *me*.

As we all know, it's a snap to give others advice, especially when we've never personally experienced a given hardship. It's easy for an Eskimo to advise a Texan on how to handle a heat wave. It's likely lousy advice, but it's easy advice.

But recently, my wife and I were faced with a personal crisis. And we were forced—she far more than I—to take our own advice.

It was the toughest thing we've ever had to do.

But I'm getting ahead of myself. Here's the back-story:

The Doctor Wants to See You Both

My wife, Carol, has always been active and fit. She watches her weight... eats healthy... weighs the same as she weighed in college... jogs... plays tennis and golf... bikes... and takes Pilates and kickboxing classes. She even ran a marathon, all 26.2 miles, through New York's Central Park when she turned 55.

She's no female Lance Armstrong, but she's fit.

In the fall of 2009, Carol visited her gynecologist for her annual checkup. She'd been experiencing some minor discomfort—abdominal cramping and the like—and subsequent tests lead her doctor to recommend a hysteroscopy to remove tissue for further diagnosis, a rather routine procedure that thousands of women undergo every day. No real cause for alarm. Surgery went smoothly, and, as is customary, some tissue was sent to the pathology lab for analysis. The surgeon asked Carol to hang around until he got the results from the lab.

Not a problem, we were in no hurry. An hour or so later a nurse asked if we'd wait a little longer: "The doctor wants to meet with both of you to discuss the results," she said. I'm not prone to overreacting, but the surgeon asking to meet with both the husband and the wife—that was a red flag. Or maybe not, I told myself. Maybe he just wanted to reassure both husband and wife that everything was fine.

I was wrong about the reassurance—everything was not fine.

"I was expecting to find a cyst, which are fairly common and usually benign," the doctor said in a soft voice. "What I found instead was a tumor in the wall of your uterus. We're sending the tissue out for further testing, but the early indications are endometrial cancer. The good news is this is a common cancer in women and is one of the more easily treatable cancers. I don't want to make light of this, but if you had to choose a cancer, this would be the one to get. It responds very well to treatment."

I don't remember much of the rest of the conversation. I could hear the doctor's words, buzzing like flies in the white waiting room. But after I heard the word "cancer," it was as if my brain was suddenly stuffed with cotton balls and wrapped in gauze. Just a few words— "cancer" and "hysterectomy"—seeped through to my consciousness like bloodstains.

Worse Than We First Thought

The surgeon suggested we make an appointment with a cancer specialist at his hospital—he recommended a few names, which I scribbled on a subscription card I pulled from a magazine in the waiting room.

It didn't take long for me to toss the list in the trash—Carol had pretty much made up her mind to have her surgery and treatment done at

Moffitt Cancer Center on the campus of the University of South Florida in Tampa, a 20-minute drive from our home. As I was backing the car out of the hospital parking garage, Carol was on her cell phone making an appointment at Moffitt. They scheduled us to meet with an OB GYN surgeon, Dr. Sachin Apte, in a couple weeks.

While we waited for the final results from the pathologists, I had accepted an invitation for the following weekend to speak to 12,000 people in the Richmond Coliseum in Richmond, Virginia, on my newest book, *Surviving the Perfect Recession*. I busied myself preparing my Power Point presentation (which I'd never done before) and writing and rehearsing my talk.

I flew into Richmond on a Friday, met with the technical staff at the coliseum to iron out any bugs in the Power Point, did a final run-through of the speech in my room, called Carol (who cheered me on and assured me I'd be a hit), and tucked in for the night.

The speech went well and the Power Point, to my great relief, went flawlessly. At the close of my talk, the crowd roared its approval (that's my version of events, and I'm sticking to it), and when I flew back into Tampa that evening, Carol picked me up at the airport, and, still pumped up over my roaring reception in Richmond, I entertained Carol with my version of the event, not noticing, in my filibuster, that Carol was more quiet than usual.

The next morning I learned why.

"Steve, after you left for Richmond, the doctor called me with the final lab results from the tissue they removed," she said as we sipped coffee over our morning paper.

"Okay...," I said distractedly, still charged up over my speech. "What did he say?"

"He said it's not just an endometrial cancer, as they first thought," she said softly. "It's a rare kind of cancer called uterine carcinosarcoma. Very aggressive and hard to treat. I did some research online. Not a history of good outcomes. The appointment at Moffitt has been moved up to Monday."

I placed the newspaper on my lap and sat silently, staring at the paper but not focusing, processing her words, feeling the tears well up and slide down my face, hearing them splash on the paper like little rain drops.

"You just broke my heart," I said in a cracked voice. I knew my statement sounded random, as if it belonged in a different conversation between a different couple. But it's all I could think to say, and I meant it.

"I found out Friday after you left," she said. "But I didn't want to tell you before your speech. I knew how important this was to you, and I didn't want to distract you."

I think I said something lame, like, "You can count on me," which I meant. But I said it flat, like a bad line in a *B* movie. We sat in silence, neither of us knowing what to say. Somebody coughed. We both cleared our throats. And then Carol broke the silence.

"I want to live the rest of my life," she said, not to me singly, but to us both. She spoke the words into the room, as a statement of fact, without a hint of self-pity or weakness of resolve. Just a statement of fact.

Her words—"I want to live the rest of my life." That's the last thing I remember about that morning. But that's okay. It's the only thing that really counts.

What Resilience Looks Like

This is a book about resilience.

And I'm going to end the book by telling you what resilience looks like. I now know firsthand what it looks like. I'm living with it. I now know that resilience has a first name.

That name is Carol.

Doctors have been treating cancer patients with chemotherapy and radiation since the end of WWII, so millions have endured the treatments, which can have harsh side effects. The treatment for Carol's cancer differed from most in that the surgeon, in her case, Dr. Apte, also headed up her chemotherapy team.

Dr. Apte appeared warm and businesslike, but not chatty. Which I liked. Save chatty for poker parties. Carol and I agreed we wanted a real professional who could make this bad thing disappear forever. She liked Dr. Apte, trusted him, and took some reassurance that his undergraduate degree in chemical engineering would be a bonus for the chemo phase.

Dr. Apte performed the hysterectomy laproscopically with the assistance of a da Vinci robot, which aids precision and minimizes the trauma. Carol spent two days in the hospital before returning home. That's when her resilience really began kicking into high gear.

When we met with Dr. Apte two weeks after the operation, I told him that only three days after her surgery, Carol had walked three miles. He looked surprised.

"You told her to walk," I said.

"Most of my patients don't walk a *total* of three miles for three years after their operation," he said with a smile.

But Carol wasn't most patients. She was committed to being actively involved in her treatment. Because carsinosarcoma is an aggressive cancer, it requires an aggressive treatment, Dr. Apte explained. The treatment involved six treatments of chemo combined with daily doses of radiation five days a week for six weeks.

During chemo, they hooked Carol up to an IV and dripped a chemical cocktail into her veins for five hours at a time. She had a total of six chemo treatments, with three-week rest periods between each treatment. The most common side effects are nausea, which Carol had none of, thank goodness; fatigue, which affects almost all patients, Carol included, especially at the tail end of her treatments; and hair loss, which started three weeks after her first chemo session.

The hair loss started gradually—a few hairs in the shower and sink. Two weeks into treatment, she started combing her hair outside in the back yard. Three weeks into treatment, she walked up to me, pointed at her head, pulled out a tuft of hair, and said, "I think it's time." She bent over the bathroom sink, whacking at her hair with scissors. Short, spiky clumps of hair remained. I suggested she use a razor to finish the job.

"Razors aren't allowed during chemo," she said. "A nick can lead to a nasty infection with my weakened immune system."

I drove to the local drug store and bought battery-powered hair clippers for $19.99. We headed into the shower, and as she bent forward, I shaved her head. I felt like a barber at a boot camp for Marines. We both cried a little, but I was more relieved than sad when I discovered she had a round head. You have no idea what a relief that was.

"If you had a zucchini head, I'd have to leave you," I joked as we swept up her hair from the shower floor. She understood. When someone you love is going through chemo, you look for the bright spots… you cling to any little surprise that lessens the grief.

Carol's round head was a big bright spot for both of us.

Attitude and Action Are Everything

For nine months, that's 270-plus days, Carol has endured pain and inconvenience and anxiety with grace and courage. She only had two brief moments of self-pity, both involving her baldness and both lasting just a few seconds. The first moment was the morning we shaved her head. That morning was tough for both of us, as the last of our denial, alongside her hair, fell to the floor in clumps. The second moment was at a drugstore, when she noticed two young boys pointing at her scarf-covered head and whispering. She said she felt like a freak for a moment. Got a bit angry. Got a bit sad. And then told herself to get over it.

"This is the price I have to pay to get healthy," she told me later. "A few years ago, what I have was a death sentence. So, I told myself that celebrations should replace sadness."

Carol refused to cave in to cancer. Eight weeks after her surgery, she went back to work and resumed her after-work exercise routine: Pilates on Monday… tennis on Tuesday… kickboxing class on Wednesday… Pilates again on Thursday… tennis Saturday morning… walking nine holes of golf with me Sunday afternoon. Oh, and a 10-mile bike ride on Saturday and Sunday, weather permitting. Plus, Carol visits her

100-year-old mother in a nursing home at least two days a week, shops for her, and does her laundry weekly. Carol also makes time to accompany her mother to doctors' appointments once or twice a month.

Resilient? That's not the word for it.

I've never once heard Carol say, "Why me?" Actually, she says the opposite. When Carol broke the news to her mother, her mom fretted, "Why not me instead of you? I've lived my life."

"Mom, I got cancer instead of you because I'm younger and stronger and can handle the chemo," Carol replied. "The treatments that would kill you will make me better."

Take Your Own Advice

When someone we know is stricken with a disease like cancer, we all weigh in with advice. I've given advice to my friends at times like these, and it's usually pretty predictable stuff. You've likely said some of the same things to friends and loved ones:

Stay positive.

Follow your doctor's orders.

Remain active and keep working to keep your mind off things.

Everything happens for a reason.

If anyone can beat this, you can.

Be strong.

You have so much to live for, so never give up hope.

They're all clichés, but they're all true. Good advice, every single one. But the trick is, when it's *your crisis…* when it's *your turn* to be on the receiving end of the advice, then you have to do what resilient people do—*take your own advice*!

That's what my wife Carol is doing—taking all the advice she's ever given or received and applying it to her challenge. Her goal is to bounce back from cancer—not to break under its onerous weight. And the best way to do that is to follow the 10 rules spelled out in this book, culminating with the last rule, taking your own advice.

Everyone is amazed at how resilient and determined Carol has been during the past nine months. They're astonished at her activity level... her positive self-talk... her quiet strength.

One of my friends e-mailed me and gushed about how strong Carol was and ended with, "She's my hero."

Carol's my hero, too. But I can do one better than that.

Carol's also my wife.